the cook's garden

Gardening Caroline Gunter

Food Karen Green

contents

Garden photography
Leigh Clapp

Food Photography
Scott Cameron

planning
for production

A cook's garden, in a world where dreams come true, supplies all of the special plants that cooks love to use. To have on hand those special textures and tastes, fresh and lush from the garden, grown as you like them, harvested at the peak of perfection and in just the quantity you need – that's what an ideal cook's garden provides.

A gardener's garden contains fine and carefully cultivated specimens of seasonal fruit and vegetables, planted in neat, regular rows, as dictated by time-honoured books, and usually cooked by equally time-honoured methods – rewarding, productive and an economic boon to the family. And there's nothing wrong with that.

But the cook's garden has more subtle supplies: a bit of this, a trial of that, a few seasonal stars, a little something happy in a pot or among the flowers. The cook's garden helps you add a bit of magic to a meal. It's that happy mix that lets you turn cooking into creation.

Your cook's garden will no doubt include many collected treasures from other cooks' gardens: some saved seeds, a piece broken off to strike or a snippet of something shared after a successful trial. Most likely there'll be seed trays, cuttings of "new" varieties in pots ready to plant into the garden proper, an assembly of herbs at the ready and various experiments with unusual shapes and colours. There's always the chance that some of these new varieties will become kitchen standards and you'll wonder how you ever lived without them.

But, of course, dreams are dreams. The dictates of climate and available space are the controllers of what becomes reality in your garden. Being able to get your hands on just the right plants can sometimes be a bit of a struggle. You'll see glorious pictures in gardening books and strange varieties in shops and wonder where on earth you will be able to get them. And then there's time, alas, so often in very short supply.

The Cook's Garden is for those ready to bridge the divide between the great kitchen indoors and the great garden outdoors, and wanting to create their own unique kitchen garden. Let's look at suggestions to help you down the garden path with your arms loaded or your fist proudly wrapped round something garden-fresh for your table.

A CONTRAST IN STYLES

LEFT A simple, but robust potager arrangement along a garden path.

ABOVE A controlled and very ornamental display in a protected walled garden.

Most design styles can become productive gardens.

THE POSSIBILITIES OF SMALL SPACES

FIRST RULE Forget the segregation of vegetables into beds. Herbs, vegetables and flowers can all be grown together for stunning visual displays. Vegetables and herbs can be beautiful in their own right, and you'll be constantly surprised at what you can achieve in small spaces.

GET RID OF THE LAWN Dig it up, removing all the roots or they'll reach up through your garden and steal valuable water and nutrients. A sea of herbs and vegetables looks twice as good as a featureless sward.

TAKE ADVANTAGE OF HEIGHT Grow climbers like peas, cucumbers and beans on tripods among floral displays. Nasturtiums can clamber among them too. Let unstaked mini tomatoes wander among tall shrubs or between stakes, for example.

MIX COLOURS The bright sparks of chillies look stunning among flowers, and the red and yellow stems of ruby chard are equally striking. Grey-leafed vegetables like artichokes, broccoli and sage extend the colour palette, so do purple-leafed beauties like beetroot, basil and beans.

MIX LEAF SHAPES AND FORMS The solid and textural greenness of silverbeet, curly-leafed kale or carrots offers a good contrast to floral colour. Lemon grass provides a wonderful grassy profile.

USE VEGETABLES AND HERBS AS BORDERS Mignonette lettuces, chives, oregano and radish make good edging plants, and team happily with violas, dwarf nasturtium and alyssum.

DON'T FORGET VERTICAL SURFACES Cover fences with wire, twine or lattice for beans, peas, chokos, cucumber, passionfruit or grapes.

DON'T LET CONCRETE DETER YOU Tiny pockets of soil can be created by building up garden beds using rocks, wood or bricks to create well-drained spots beside steps or even straight onto concrete. Such raised beds will happily accommodate herbs, and with frequent watering and nourishment, small lettuce, rocket or Asian greens.

dictates of climate

Choosing the wrong plants for your climate will make gardening much more difficult than it actually is.

Of course we all want to grow a lemon or a lime, quinces or nuts, asparagus or raspberries, passionfruit or mangoes, things that tempt us, but in reality are climatically impossible. Some of us will even take up the challenge, attempt to create the right microclimate with wind, shade or sun barriers, even moving large pots about. And sometimes we succeed, but more often it's a huge struggle for, most likely, a meagre result.

It is much wiser to accept the limitations of your particular garden conditions and choose those herbs and vegetables that grow well. You'll find that, in any climate range, you will still have considerable choice of fruits, herbs, flowers and vegetables. Seek out those plants that provide flavour, texture or colour contrasts. Study successful gardens in your area to see what works well and adopt what you like. Talk to local gardeners.

This way, you'll find your garden will be much more successful, and seasonal variation, rather than a limitation, will become a welcome delight.

dictates of space

Some lucky gardeners have large vegetable plots with space for everything. Make no mistake, though, such gardens are a lot of work, both in preparation and maintenance. Other gardeners take advantage of tiny spaces – a patch of concrete, a balcony, a collection of pots – and still grow delicious vegetables and herbs, things a cook needs to add a special flavour, a decorative flourish and that home-grown touch.

A cook's garden can be as large or as small as you have space, time and the inclination for working in it. Also, when time is short, a small garden can be infinitely more rewarding and successful than a large, ambitious garden that takes up so much time and energy that it is often abandoned. Make the most of your space.

year-round harvest

Undoubtedly, one of the genuine joys of home gardening is the thrill of enjoying fruit and vegetables in season at their best. Supermarket shopping has dulled and denied our appreciation of such gastronomic thrills as new-season pears and peaches, fresh baby potatoes, oranges in winter and freshly picked ears of corn.

A carefully designed cook's garden, however small, can yield favourite fruits and vegetables for a varied and colourful seasonal table. The enthusiastic cook with a kitchen garden at the ready will rise to the cooking challenge and explore the wonderful world of fresh herbs and home-grown produce.

LEFT A pot of parsley and basil stands by the kitchen door with a pot of mizuna and loose-leaf lettuce varieties handy.

plant supplies

The easiest way to acquire seeds and plants is, of course, to buy them from local nurseries. This way, you'll always buy what's in season for your area. Choose the healthiest looking plants; green, not lanky or leaning; still growing robustly and not in flower.

It's also easy to raise seeds from packets. Use a special seed-raising mix and in cold, frosty climates, start seedlings early indoors or under glass.

There are many mail-order companies that supply seeds, and the variety of choice is exciting. Some specialise in unusual or heirloom varieties, and so in your cook's garden you can experiment with, amongst others, rare and unusual tomatoes, pumpkins, Swiss chard and beans. Seeds are inexpensive and there is much delight to be gained from raising and nurturing little-known vegetables and experimenting with colours and striking leaf shapes.

The other means of acquiring seeds is to save your own seeds from the last year's harvest (provided of course they are not hybrid forms) and the seeds will germinate next year. In doing this, you will be partaking in an age-old horticultural practice, keeping alive rare varieties, and your favourite tomatoes, pumpkins and beans will be yours forever.

Gardening is also a great way of sharing. Gardeners love to swap stories, wisdom, experiences, old wives' tales, seeds and seedlings. Don't worry if you raise too many seedlings or have leftovers from punnets as there is usually someone nearby to share in your enthusiasm for gardening.

AND THEN THERE ARE POTS

Make sure you choose pots that are big enough to easily hold the mass of roots that are to fill them, or they'll be forever thirsty and weak. They need to be 10cm (4") wider and deeper than the root ball.

Terracotta is impressive but expensive. Plastic pots are cheap. They don't dry out as quickly, but will blow over and deteriorate with exposure to the sun. Any metal or wooden container like a bucket, wheel-barrow or half-barrel will do a perfect job as a pot, but must have holes for drainage. Wooden crates and polystyrene boxes have been successfully used for vegie plots.

Most trees will grow in pots but not to full size because their roots are restricted. Citrus trees are often potted. Olives are very content to grow in pots, so too are guavas and bay. Miniature varieties of apples, peach, nectarine and cherries are also ideal. They all need careful maintenance.

Herbs make excellent potted plants as most love good drainage. Choose pots that suit their shape: tall herbs like dill, rosemary or tarragon look good in tall, wide pots; weeping types like thyme or savory are better suited to cascading on their own over pots 15–20cm (6–8") high, or as borders to the mound-shaped sage, parsley, basil or marjoram. Mint, standard and Vietnamese varieties, is best confined to a pot because it's so invasive, and chervil can be moved into semi-shade during the hottest part of the year.

Tomatoes, especially the mini varieties, make excellent pot specimens, but demand large pots to accommodate their root systems. Capsicums, cucumbers, chillies, all the leafy green crops and beans will do well in pots, as will the winter vegetables like broccoli or mini cauliflower and peas.

See care and maintenance, pages 7–8.

cultivation
for success

CLEARING AND PLANTING IN A SINGLE BLOW

WORM FARMS

Worm farms are a form of kitchen and garden waste recycling. They put to good use the incredible ability of earth worms to digest and decompose organic matter. You will need a three-layered stack of plastic trays (available as a kit from hardware shops and garden supplies) and a large supply of worms. It's an odour-free and efficient way to recycle kitchen waste. The upper layer houses the worms in moist peat beds and here you add kitchen refuse, vegetable peelings, leftovers, shredded paper, coffee grains, tea leaves, leaf debris from the garden etc. (Worms don't like onion and citrus skins and meat waste.) The second layer collects the worm castings or vermipost, the nutrient-rich by-product of their digestive processes. This can be spread over the garden as mulch or used to raise seedlings. The bottom layer collects an equally valuable liquid which can be used as a liquid fertiliser, neat for established plants or diluted to half strength for seedlings. Recycling at its best.

soil types

Yes, alas, you have to cultivate.

There's no denying the major requirement for success with producing crops is the condition of your soil. There are two major soil types: clay and sand, and your soil will be at one or the other of these two ends of the scale, or somewhere in between, where the quantities of sand, clay and organic material are mixed. Clay is fine-particled, hard when dry and sticky when wet. It will clump onto your shoes and your garden fork and stay there, moulded into shape. Clay soils have good supplies of the minerals and essential elements for plant growth but little space for air, water, and the roots to move through. To break up these heavy soils, spread on gypsum (available from your nursery or agricultural supply store), leave for a month, then dig in large quantities of organic matter, like compost and manure. A short-cut technique is to spread gypsum, add a layer of pelleted poultry manure and then build a garden bed on top of this, raised enough to allow room for root growth. Use garden soil mix, well-aged manure and compost mixed together. This is all you need to grow the first crop. The following season it can be dug in and combined with the underlying clay. Add more organic supplies each season. But don't dig these soils when they're wet (they'll stick into clods) or when too dry (you'll become exhausted and the fine soil particles will blow away in the wind). Soil that is just moist is easiest and best to dig.

Sand has large particles visible to the naked eye. The soil will not compact, even when squeezed. Air (essential for the roots), fills the gaps, but water (essential for the whole plant) drains away too rapidly. To slow down the rate of water loss and to increase the nutrient- and mineral-holding capacity of the sand, add large quantities of manure and well-rotted compost.

The middle group, the loams, are sand or clay mixed with enough organic material to make them workable, and are the ideal garden soil. But even they need regular applications of the organic duo if they are to remain productive.

fertilisers

Vegetables fall into three groups: leafy types, flowering/fruiting varieties and root crops. They all have their own preferences for essential elements.

• Leafy vegetables and herbs (for example, spinach, lettuce, basil, cabbage) need large amounts of nitrogen (N) for vigorous growth and abundant foliage.

• Flowering/fruiting varieties are those that grow a container of seeds (for example, peas, pumpkin, cucumbers and tomatoes). Their special requirement is potassium (K) to boost flowering.

• Root vegetables require good supplies of phosphorus (P) for vigorous root development.

To supply these needs we have two choices of fertiliser: chemical or organic.

CHEMICAL FERTILISERS are constructed artificially by combining elements to correct specific problems like magnesium, phosphorus or potassium deficiencies, or mixed to suit specific plant varieties. There are also complete plant foods, with a mix of all the elements for healthy plant growth. These are the most suitable for vegetable growth. They are mixed into the soil before planting time to avoid chemical burning of seedling roots. There are mixes that are diluted in water for quick-acting foliar sprays. Slow-release pelleted formulas are a more gentle method of providing nutrients, and less likely to shock plants.

For all of them, use only the quantities recommended on the package as overload will kill plants. The only additional need is nitrogen boosts in liquid dressings for leafy vegetables.

ORGANIC FERTILISERS provide required elements in natural form and will not build up deposits of unused chemical salts in the soil. They are available as slow-release pelleted poultry manure (with a nutrient composition similar to the complete plant foods) or blood and bone, bone dust, linseed, cottonseed, and castor meal. All organic fertilisers are slow-release formulas as they must decompose before the nutrients are available. Seaweed and fish emulsions are foliar organic sprays and there are other manure- or plant-derived mixes that can be blended at home. Their nutrients are available immediately.

MANURES are not fertilisers but soil improvers. They help provide the light, airy composition required but their nutrient benefits are low. Manures must be well decomposed before seedlings are put in as the process of breaking down can kill the plants. Spread it on the garden a month before planting or spread out in sunlight until it loses its strong aroma. It's then safe to use.

There are other soil conditions, like acidity or alkalinity (its pH), that influence how plants grow. In most gardens the soil pH is not a problem but by varying the sources of organic matter used, you'll prevent any imbalances developing. Should problems arise, take a soil sample to your nursery.

potted plants
planting out pots

Good soil and constant watering are essential, no matter what pot you use. Normal garden soil can't be used. Well-matured compost is OK but reduces in volume and requires topping up. Commercial potting mixes are the other alternative. Buy the best you can afford.

NO-DIG GARDENS

A very productive form of gardening but it does require heavy work to set up. It can be used for problems like weed-ridden, rocky or severely compacted soils, and even over concrete. Wood, bricks, garden walling and sleepers can be used to frame a garden bed. The bed must be strong enough to bear the weight of wet fillings and 1.2m (4') high to accommodate roots.

soil-based sites

Build up the following layers:
1 light cover of pelleted poultry manure
2 5cm (2") layer of damp newspaper
3 complete layer of lucerne hay "biscuits" 5cm (2") thick and flaked off the bale
4 10cm (4") layer of chicken manure
5 20cm (8") thick layer of straw
6 another layer of pelleted poultry manure
7 10cm (4") layer of rich compost.

Water well and add pockets of extra compost when adding plants.

concrete or paved sites

Start with a 5cm (2") layer of gravel for drainage, then add layers 3–6, above. Repeat the layers until the garden is 2–3cm (2") below the top of the bed.

Do not dig and disturb the layers. Place plants into extra compost pockets and keep the bed well watered. After each harvest, add compost to top-up but eventually replace the whole structure when the level falls low enough to fit in layers 3–7.

RAISED BEDS ON A DIFFICULT SITE

COMPANION PLANTING

Some plants grow better if you plant them alongside each other. United, they support, shelter and provide root space and nutrients for each other. Some herbs deter insect pests. In kitchen gardens this is great news. A careful selection of plants and companions means that you can grow much variety within a small space while at the same time you help control pests. Nor are insect infestations likely to reach plague proportions as they can easily do in larger, single-crop garden beds.

Here are some well-known plant combinations:

BEANS grow more strongly with summer savory and when planted alternately with corn.

CABBAGE, CAULIFLOWER AND BROCCOLI get protection from cabbage moth when near celery, sage or rosemary.

CALENDULA attract hover flies which eat aphids on peas or broad beans.

NASTURTIUMS repel aphids among the peas and beetles among pumpkins and cucumbers.

POTATOES are more disease-resistant when planted among horseradish and, when planted with beans, are less likely to suffer beetle damage.

TOMATOES have more flavour when grown near basil and will develop more vigorously near marigolds.

Gravel or pottery shards in the base of a pot improve drainage. Put in a 10–15cm (4–6") layer of potting mix over the base, place the root ball on top, fill around the sides and add a light layer of potting mix. The plant should sit 2.5cm (1") below the rim. Add slow-release fertiliser at the recommended rate and later, regular light sprays with a foliage fertiliser to keep plants robust.

re-potting

For small pots, replace the mix for each new planting. For large pots, dig the soil well and add fertiliser and top-ups of compost to keep the mix light.

Re-pot your plants when they become root-bound. If small enough to handle, pull the dampened plant from the pot and carve away some of the roots. Replace in new potting mix and prune to keep the top and bottom in proportion. Water well and start the fertiliser regime 2 weeks later.

watering pots

It's so easy to forget. They dry out very quickly and you'll come home to dead treasures on the doorstep. If you're busy, a watering system is a great boon, and friendly neighbours are essential when you go away. Don't stand pots permanently in water-filled saucers as their roots rot. It can be an emergency measure for weekends away, but take them out as soon as you return.

crop rotation

Rotating crops makes the nutrients added by one plant available to subsequent plants. For example, legumes trap nitrogen in nodules on their roots. Leafy vegetables, which need large quantities of nitrogen, will benefit from the added nitrogen if planted after legumes. Likewise, root vegetables planted after leafy vegetables will utilise the phosphorus not needed by the leafy vegetables. Fruiting plants such as tomatoes, peas, cucumbers and the like will make use of spare potassium.

Crop rotating ensures soil-living pests and diseases favouring one plant group cannot build up in the one spot. Gardening in this manner, though requiring planning and knowledge, means that all the nutrients in the soil are used and the garden is worked to maximum effect.

pests and diseases

Alas, they turn up. The first step in managing garden pests is to accurately diagnose them. Infestations of leaf-eating insects are easy to identify. Caterpillars can be found on or under leaves making inroads into them. Some beetles chew leaves as well.

Chemical sprays will kill insects and unwanted pests, but can be harmful to humans and beneficial insects. It's wiser to kill them by hand (possible in a kitchen garden) or treat with safe sprays like garlic spray (see instructions, opposite page) or use pyrethrum-based alternatives or, for caterpillars, Dipel, a bio-insecticide with low toxicity.

Chemical baits are available for slugs and snails, as are safer, organic alternatives. Gather them by hand at night and tread on them or drown them in a mix of water and detergent, kill them as they drink from saucers of alcohol or milk, or make barriers of sawdust or grit.

Sap-sucking insects range from minute dots (thrip), to moving masses (aphids), static hard pinheads (scales), small flies (white fly) to beetles (stink bugs). There are commercial chemical treatments for all of these, but if you wish to remain organic, crush by hand where possible, blast off with water or try garlic spray or chilli spray (see instructions, this page).

Other leaf problems include fungus, mildew and rust. They cover and eventually kill leaves. Commercial sprays will save the plant if used early enough and stop the spread of spores. Alternative treatments include bicarbonate of soda spray or milk spray (see instructions, this page).

Soil fungus can be reduced in small areas by pouring on boiling water prior to planting. Check that the soil is not full of active worms.

Collect stem-eating grubs in the soil during the day and at night when active on the surface. Marigolds repel grubs and nematodes for several metres.

Fruit-fly need special attention. Chemical treatments should be used to stop their spread. Alternative treatments include Dak pots and home-made traps made from PET bottles filled with sweetened wine or sherry. Empty and refill regularly. Don't leave dropped fruit on the ground where the fruit-fly larvae pupate. Collect and boil, or seal in plastic bags and "cook" any damaged fruit in the sun.

compost

Compost is a very effective system for recycling and reducing garden waste; it reproduces in the garden what happens in nature where vegetable matter decomposes and returns to the soil.

There is no mystery about composting. You can, if you want, simply pile waste on open ground and wait. However, the whole process is sped up if you build a wooden- or wire-sided container 1m (3') high. Make sure your compost pile is in the sun, there is earth beneath, air and water can penetrate and there is easy access. Add kitchen waste, non-diseased garden waste, shredded paper, even hair and vacuum cleaner contents. The rule is that if it was once alive, it's suitable to compost. Avoid bones and meat waste as they encourage scavengers and flies. Between each addition, add layers of lawn clippings or leaves. Herbs (comfrey, yarrow and tansy) and blood and bone will speed up the process. When full, the pile can be turned and left to mature. You can then begin a new compost pile and the original will be useable in 3–4 months.

Plastic bins with lids are recommended for city gardens as they take up less space, don't attract vermin and don't look unsightly. Also available is a barrel that is tumbled daily. This method is faster than plastic bins or open piles.

PHOTO: SCOTT CAMERON

HOME-MADE SPRAYS

garlic spray

- Soak 100g chopped garlic in 2 tablespoons mineral oil or liquid paraffin for 48 hours.
- Add 2 cups (500ml) hot water and 30g pure soap.
- Cool and strain finely. Lumps will clog the spray nozzle.
- Store in glass or plastic, clearly labelled.
- To use, dilute 3 teaspoons in 4 cups (1 litre) water for spraying.

chilli spray

- Blend a large handful of fresh chillies in 2 cups (500ml) hot water.
- Add $1/2$ cup of pure soap flakes.
- Cool and strain finely.
- Store clearly labelled and dilute 4 teaspoons in 4 cups (1 litre) water.
- Spray on leaves or dribble neat on ant trails and around infested pots.

bicarbonate of soda spray

- Mix together 2g bicarbonate of soda and 2 teaspoons pure soap flakes in 4 cups (1 litre) hot water.
- Cool and spray weekly on leaves.

milk spray

- Combine 2 cups (500ml) milk in 4 cups (1 litre) water. Spray regularly.

Spring

PLEASANT SEASONAL CHORE

Spring
garden diary

Spring is the season of anticipation.

Even though the calendar may announce its arrival, often the weather does not. We usually get the odd hot spring day, a foretaste of languid summer making us anticipate its delights, and then on the next day there's a sharp, cold reminder to bring us back to reality. However, it's the lengthening daylight hours that summer-growing plants respond to, so don't despair if chilly winds blow.

Plants start to grow because they have to; they've been beckoned. The leaves and buds unfurl with splashes of subtle colour, and the full display of spring flowers strengthens as the season takes hold. In a corner of the vegetable garden, asparagus responds to the directive, bees are heard among the peas, and the broad beans flower. Tarragon and chives obey the command and wave their leaves in the breeze like banners.

If space is not a problem, leave garden beds fallow over winter, covered in manure and mulch. They will be ready for planting in spring. Areas shaded in winter are best revitalised in this way.

Most city gardens don't have the luxury of space. To make room for spring, clear existing beds, remove ragged, tired-looking plants that are no longer productive and above all be inventive with plant combinations and space-saving ideas. Compost all debris. Chop up tough stems to speed up decomposition.

Save wizened bean or pea pods and store for the next sowing. Dig up clods and break up roots in the soil. Add well-rotted compost.

Early-bird gardeners will have already raised tomato, basil, capsicum and zucchini seedlings under cover during late winter or been down to the local nursery for seedlings. Gardeners in frost-prone areas must time their planting out carefully to avoid tricky, late frosts.

Now, your most difficult gardening decision is whether to plant favourites or new varieties. All are worth a try. Remember, good soil preparation, combination planting and crop rotation will ensure an abundant and wonderfully diverse kitchen garden.

pick now...

MOST GARDENS

- beetroot
- broccoli
- broad beans
- cabbage
- cauliflower
- endive
- leeks
- lettuce
- onion
- peas
- radicchio
- rhubarb
- silverbeet
- spinach

TEMPERATE AND COOL GARDENS

- asparagus

plant now...

SUBTROPICAL AND MEDITERRANEAN GARDENS

- beans
- capsicum
- chilli
- choko
- cucumber
- carrot
- eggplant
- lettuce
- melons
- potatoes
- radish
- sweet corn
- tomatoes
- zucchini

TEMPERATE GARDENS

- asparagus
- broad beans
- cabbage
- leeks
- peas
- and any of the above as frosts cease

TROPICAL GARDENS

- okra

CLOCKWISE FROM TOP LEFT Beware of spiders crawling into gloves and boots
left lying around; a productive garden with a protective bird barrier above;
the attractive flower head of garlic; potting up parsley.

garden peas

AN "OCTOPOD" OF STICKS SUPPORTS
CLIMBING PEAS

PRESERVING THE CROP

STORING All peas should be eaten as soon
as possible after picking. If they must
be stored, rinse and dry thoroughly
on absorbent paper and store in the
refrigerator. Don't pod peas until you
are ready to cook them.

FREEZING An oversupply of green peas
can be blanched and frozen (see Freezing,
page 117). More than one child has been
known to snack on frozen peas. Sugar
snap peas and snow peas do not freeze
well; but a pea puree will, so cook the
peas, puree and then freeze.

You might consider it useless growing peas at home, when the frozen
alternative is so convenient. But the flavour of a just-picked pea
makes it all worthwhile. Like sweet corn, peas have a high sugar content
which slowly converts to starch after picking. If you gather peas young and
eat them straight off the bush, you can really taste the difference.

Today's gardener can grow many kinds of peas. Snow peas (or mange tout)
and sugar snap peas are now as well known as regular green peas. Also try
unusual varieties like wrinkled peas, said to have superior flavour and
winged, or asparagus, peas for something completely different. In a small
kitchen garden, you'll be able to grow enough for a small harvest once or
twice a week; in a large garden you'll have supplies to freeze or give away.

in the garden

In cool temperate gardens peas grow almost all year round. They need some
shade when the sun is hot. The plants are frost-tolerant but the flowers and
young pods are not, so avoid winter frosts. In warmer gardens, peas make a
useful winter crop; in tropical gardens plant after the wet to avoid mildew.

Prepare a well-drained and sunny site by digging over well. As weed removal
is difficult between seedlings, a mulch mat on either side of the rows or in
the centre and around the outside of a tripod should help. Leave a 2cm (1")
gap for the seeds. Put down slow-release fertiliser or blood and bone and
cover it with a 3cm (1¹/₄") thick layer of damp newspaper, spreading 10cm (4")
beyond the seed position. Gravel or lucerne will hide it and stop it blowing
away. The weeds can't break through until the paper disintegrates and the
pea roots can reach the fertiliser right through their growth. Put in stakes
and wire or twine for row planting, and tripod supports and connecting twine
if growing in teepee shapes. Peas grow 2m (6') high.

Wet the soil and plant the seeds 5cm (2") deep so birds and mice won't find
them, spacing them about 10cm (4") apart if they are to grow up frames or
poles, closer if they are to be self-supporting on the ground. The seedlings
will break through in about a week, taking longer if the soil is cool.

Water regularly after the seedlings emerge. Flowers will start in a couple of
months and pods a week later. Don't let the pods grow too big as the peas will
be mealy and the plants will stop producing. The more you pick, the more the
plants produce. Peas for shelling should have space between each pea and the
pod shouldn't be tight. Peas eaten in the pod (snow peas and sugar snap peas)
should be pliable, about 8cm (3–4") long with small pea formations visible.

At the end of the season, cut off the stems at ground level and compost undiseased stems and leaves. Leave the roots and their nitrogen nodules in the ground for a crop of lettuce or silverbeet to use.

pests and diseases

Problems include aphids. Hose off, crush between your fingers or spray with pyrethrum sprays. Another problem is mildew which can kill pea plants. Use a commercial spray or try our bicarbonate of soda spray (see page 9) which won't harm bees, peas or predators.

for the table

to prepare...

~ Sugar snap peas and snow peas need very little cooking. Add to boiling water and cook until they just change colour. If they are for salads, remove and cool in iced water.

~ Green peas require slightly more cooking and the older the peas, the longer time required, generally about 2–4 minutes. Don't overcook as this toughens peas. NEVER add bicarbonate of soda to the water. The peas stay green, but you destroy their nutritional value.

to serve...

~ Fresh pea soup is fantastic! Cook peas in chicken stock and blend with the pulp from a roasted bulb of garlic. Stir in cream or more chicken stock, if necessary. Add snipped chives, salt and pepper. Serve chilled or hot.

~ Secure blanched snow peas around cooked prawns with toothpicks and serve with a soy-chilli dipping sauce.

~ Serve green peas, sugar snap peas and snow peas tossed through a little gremolata (a mixture of garlic, lemon rind and parsley).

~ Fry some fine bacon strips until crisp, add a little balsamic vinegar and some blanched sugar snap peas.

~ Both sugar snap peas and snow peas, when lightly blanched, can be used as crudités, particularly good with bagna cauda, the Italian anchovy sauce.

~ For a spring salad, toss any blanched pea with lettuce, asparagus tips, spring onions, chervil and parsley leaves; dress with a vinaigrette and add crumbled blue cheese.

Dinner becomes something more than grilled fish or chicken with this simple pea sauce (particularly good with Atlantic salmon). Cook some peas in a light chicken stock until very soft; sieve and thin with more chicken stock, if necessary. Season

potatoes

JUST WASH AND COOK

R are is the person who doesn't eat potatoes, whether as the ubiquitous chip, comforting mashed spuds or via more sophisticated cooking methods. Nor is a potato merely a potato these days. A shopping trip means negotiating the unfamiliar names of pontiac, desiree, pink fir, kipfler and King Edward, all with their different textures, tastes and colours.

Few gardeners, though, ever grow potatoes. They are well worth the effort as each kind has its own distinctive flavour and texture. Potatoes are easy to propagate. You simply keep a few of your favourite varieties, let them sprout and grow your own. All you really need is a sunny, well-drained site and enough room.

in the garden

Potatoes must be grown in frost-free conditions, so wait until there's no risk of late frosts. They can be planted all year where winter conditions are mild. In tropical areas, don't plant them in the "wet" as they'll rot.

Select a sunny, well-drained position. If the soil was not manured for the previous crop, add compost so the soil is light. Break up heavy clods. Don't add lime, but do add a complete or slow-release organic fertiliser.

Potatoes grow from whole potatoes or small pieces (golf-ball size) that have started to sprout. You can sprout your own (just keep until shoots form) or buy seed potatoes from nurseries (guaranteed virus-free, which is important if you've had dieback problems with potatoes or related crops such as tomatoes, capsicum and eggplant).

Make a furrow about 15cm (6") deep and position the potato pieces about 40cm (16") apart, with their "eyes" or sprouts facing up. Backfill with fine soil and mulch to reduce weeds and late-frost damage.

When the leafy stems are about 20cm (8") tall, hill up the soil to about 5cm (2") below the top of the stem on each plant, creating furrows between them. Hilling encourages more stems to develop and hence more potatoes. It also prevents light reaching the potato tubers – when exposed to light they turn green and are poisonous. Potatoes need regular watering to keep the tubers well-shaped and smooth-skinned. Use the furrow to irrigate your crop and make harvesting easier. If space is limited, you can also plant potatoes in tyres or log beds. Add new tyres or extra logs with a further dressing of soil each time the stems elongate.

New potatoes are ready to harvest when the flowers are fully open, about 12 weeks after planting, and the tubers are about the size of hen eggs.

PRESERVING THE CROP

STORING Potatoes should be stored in a cool, dark, airy place. Remove "eyes" as they appear and the life of your potatoes will be extended. Refrigerating potatoes converts the starches to sugar, causing them to become sweet. Direct sunlight produces a green skin – these potatoes should not be eaten.

FREEZING Fresh potatoes are not suitable for freezing.

In Australia, the term "bandicooting" refers to scrabbling about under the plants to gather just enough for each meal, just as the native namesake does. Unlike this animal, you can investigate without destroying the root connections and leave undersized tubers to fatten up later.

If you leave potatoes longer, they develop their familiar hard skins and so can be stored. Harvest when the foliage has browned. Lift gently with a fork or with your hands to avoid damage. Shake off the soil and dry for a few hours out of the sunlight. Give them a rumble to remove excess soil, then store in an airy basket, hessian bag or box in the dark, away from pests.

for the table

to prepare…

~ A common mistake is to boil potatoes covered. This results in a messy stove-top. Instead, just cover potato pieces with water, bring to the boil and cook uncovered for 10–15 minutes until soft.

~ Potatoes cook perfectly in the microwave. When cooking whole, pierce the skins all over with a fork, dampen the potatoes, cover with microwave-safe plastic wrap and cook in 5-minute intervals until soft when tested with a skewer. Potatoes pieces need a shorter cooking time.

~ Wedges don't have to mean high fat. Place peeled potatoes in a pan of cold water and bring to the boil; remove from the heat and let stand for 5 minutes. Drain and cool until they can be handled. Cut each potato into 6–8 wedges. Place 2–3 tablespoons of vegetable oil in a bowl, add the wedges and rub all over with oil. Place the wedges on a large baking tray, sprinkle with sea salt and chopped herbs, if you like. Bake in a moderately hot oven for about 30 minutes until the wedges are starting to crisp. Turn only once.

~ For creamy, delicious mashed potatoes, peel and cut potatoes into small pieces. Cover with cold milk. Bring to the boil and cook until soft but not falling apart. Drain, reserving any milk, then mash in the same pan, adding the reserved milk and a little butter if desired. Season with salt and pepper.

~ The secret of the perfect chip is frying them twice and sprinkling with salt as soon as they leave the oil – not 5 minutes later. Dry potatoes on a clean tea-towel or paper towel before frying and always use hot, clean oil.

to serve…

~ The creamy texture of boiled baby new potatoes, with just a sprinkle of sea salt, is loved by all.

~ Potatoes carry the flavourings of the ingredients they're cooked with; they can extend a meal and make tasty snacks, lunches and breakfasts.

~ If you've never tried grated potato cakes with smoked salmon, sour cream and dill with a glass of chilled champagne first thing in the morning, then you haven't lived.

herbed baby potatoes

Serve hot as a side dish or at room temperature as a salad. The potatoes will be more crisp if served hot. Choose the herb to suit the meal, eg rosemary with lamb, sage with pork etc.

1kg baby new potatoes

1 tablespoon olive oil

60g butter

2 cloves garlic, crushed

2 tablespoons fresh rosemary, tarragon, thyme or sage, chopped

salt and pepper to taste

PLACE POTATOES in a large pan, cover with cold water and bring to the boil. Remove from heat and let stand in hot water for 5 minutes. Drain and cool until they can be handled. Cut each potato in half. Heat oil and butter in a large frying pan; add potatoes, cut-side down. Cover and cook over a medium-high heat for 10 minutes or until the cut surface is golden and crisp. Add the garlic and cook for further 5 minutes. Sprinkle herbs over the potatoes and toss gently. Season with lots of cracked black pepper and sea salt, if you like.

Serves 4–6.

onions

"STORING" SHOP-BOUGHT GREEN ONIONS

Onions must be one of the most widely used vegetables of all. They feature in every cuisine. For the gardening cook, to grow your own seems an impossible task for to be self-sufficient in onions you'd need a small farm. However, unusual and special-purpose onions are worth the effort and the little space they require in a kitchen garden. They are easy to grow and you'll have some bunching varieties for life. Onions store well in dry conditions and tiny onions are easily pickled.

in the garden

The soil for all bulb crops needs to be light and well dug so the roots can penetrate. It must also be well drained to prevent rot. If there are any hard clay clods, dig in coarse sand and fine organic material to open it up. Mix it in well.

Should you have a hard clay base near the surface, raise the bed by mounding it over with garden mix or very fine compost. Sprinkle blood and bone or a complete fertiliser over the surface and rake in. Make shallow furrows only 0.5cm (1/4") deep and sprinkle in the selected seeds. Cover with compost or seed-raising mixture. Water well. If planting seedlings, place 10cm (4") apart.

bulb onions

To grow onions that will develop into bulbs, you need to select the appropriate seed. "Early" or winter-growing onions are sown at the start of autumn to give you white spring onion shapes in, surprisingly, spring. These

PHOTO: SCOTT CAMERON

BROWN, WHITE AND RED ONIONS

can be also pickled and used in dishes requiring whole small onions. "Mid" and "late" season onions are planted in mid-autumn or late autumn and are harvested in summer after their leaves have dried out. Varieties include white, red and brown onions. These slow-maturers, after drying in the sun, are the best for storage.

green onions

Green onions (scallions or bunching onions) can be planted all year round in subtropical and tropical climates, and all but mid-winter in temperate and cold gardens. Buy seed specific to this crop. They can be harvested in 8–12 weeks. For continuous supplies, repeat the planting every 4–6 weeks.

Here is a labour-saving (cheat's) technique for cultivating green onions. When a recipe calls for green onions and you've bought a bunch, you'll probably have some left over. Trim their stems by half and plant as a bunch, just covering the roots. They'll continue to grow and be waiting for the next time you need some. They certainly won't turn into those soggy disappointments you find in the bottom of the refrigerator.

unusual varieties

There are a few unusual onion varieties that home gardeners might like to try as they are both versatile and productive and take up little space. They are all multiplier onions; that is, they develop clusters of bulbs.

GOLDEN (OR FRENCH) SHALLOTS are expensive and often difficult to buy. Small bulbs can be grown at home, either from seeds but more often bought as sets or a bulb cluster. The bulbs are separated and pushed 5–7cm (2–3") deep into the soil, 15cm (6") apart in autumn or early winter. They'll multiply rapidly and you'll be able to lift them in 3–4 months. Store in a dry place and keep enough for next season's planting. They don't appreciate very wet or humid conditions.

POTATO ONIONS, like golden shallots, expand their clusters of bulblets underground after planting in autumn. The bulbs expand as well as multiply. Harvest in spring or summer before the humidity rots them.

TREE OR EGYPTIAN ONIONS grow from bulbs planted in autumn and multiply underground. They also produce many small onions at the top of the flower stalks. If not gathered, these weigh down the stem until it touches the ground where they root and start a new cluster.

WELSH (OR, MORE CORRECTLY, JAPANESE) BUNCHING ONIONS are also called ever-ready onions and are perhaps the most useful small onions of all. In a well-drained sunny spot they will remain evergreen throughout the year and the leaves and stems can be cut and used like chives or green onions. To harvest, break off what you require and push the soil back around the clump. If the clump is too tightly packed, lift it with a fork, break off the excess and replant. The cluster will continually expand and will need dividing every couple of years to provide new space and soil to grow into.

GOLDEN SHALLOTS

SPRING ONIONS

PHOTOS: SCOTT CAMERON

GREEN ONIONS

PRESERVING THE CROP

STORING Brown and white onions should be stored in a cool, dark, airy place. Red onions and the sweeter yellow onions store for longer in the refrigerator. Spring onions and green onions should be trimmed as little as possible and stored, wrapped in a damp tea-towel, in a plastic bag in the refrigerator. Ideally, use straight from the garden. Bought green onions can be planted in the garden or even a pot until they are needed; they last for months and there is no waste.

FREEZING Onions from the garden can be peeled, chopped and frozen for up to 3 months (see Freezing, page 117) in well-sealed plastic bags. Small onions can be frozen whole if peeled and blanched. Seal well so they don't spoil other food in the freezer. Onions can be gently fried, with or without garlic, and frozen for up to a month to give you a head start for busy, mid-week dinners.

PICKLING To pickle small onions or shallots, salt peeled onions overnight, rinse and pack into sterilised glass jars (see Bottling, page 118), adding a few spices such as cloves, peppercorns and dried chillies as you go. Pour over warmed vinegar (malt, white or cider) to cover. For sweeter pickled onions, dissolve ¹/₂ cup (110g) sugar in 4 cups (1 litre) of vinegar. Seal the jars and store in a cool, dark place for 3–4 weeks before opening.

for the table

to prepare...

⌒ The biggest problem with onions, as we all know, is that they make our eyes water. Various remedies have been proposed: wearing goggles, holding a spoon in your mouth, only chopping onions on the full moon after midnight. The only tried and true way to avoid weeping is to get someone else to cut onions for you. So, the next time guests ask if they can help ...

⌒ For a dish where the shape of the onion pieces doesn't matter (such as stuffing for poultry), use a food processor. It's quicker and prevents the tears.

⌒ When cooking onions with a roast dinner, cut in half and thread them through the un-cut sides onto skewers. They will be easy to turn and the centres won't pop out.

to serve...

⌒ The smell of onions on a barbecue can incite the neighbourhood. For perfect onions, slice them thickly, put them in a heatproof bowl and pour over enough boiling water to cover. Let stand for about 15 minutes, drain and pat dry. Toss in some vegetable oil and cook as usual. They can be prepared several hours ahead, covered and stored at room temperature.

⌒ Sliced onion and tomato salad, drizzled with cider vinegar and olive oil, sprinkled with sugar and left to stand for about 30 minutes is also an old favourite. Try adding watermelon with a few olives and a sprinkle of shredded fresh parsley.

⌒ This delicious onion sauce is easy, can be prepared ahead and goes well with grilled, roast or pan-fried pork. Heat some olive oil in a heavy-based pan; add some sliced onions, cover and reduce the heat to low, cook for about 20 minutes stirring occasionally. When very soft and golden add some peeled, sliced apples, several crushed juniper berries, apple juice and a splash of gin. Cook, uncovered, for about 15 minutes or until the apples are soft and most of the liquid has evaporated. This sauce keeps well, covered, in the refrigerator for several days, or can be frozen for up to a month.

⌒ Glazed golden shallots are beautiful to look at as well as to eat. Cook peeled shallots in a little oil and garlic over low heat, covered, for about 20 minutes or until very soft. Remove the lid and add some stock, bring to the boil and boil, uncovered, until the stock has almost evaporated. Add a little sugar to the stock for sweeter glazed onions, if you prefer. Serve as an accompaniment.

⌒ Make a quick Thai salad using finely shredded red onions, whole mint leaves and wedges of Roma tomatoes. Dress with a mixture of fish sauce, lime juice and a touch of palm sugar. Add some shredded cooked chicken, rare roast beef or flaked poached fish to make a main course. For those who like it hot, add some shredded chillies or a touch of sweet chilli sauce.

onion tart

This pastry is very easy and good for any savoury tart,
but you can also use frozen ready-rolled pastry sheets,
joined with a little egg yolk.

5 large onions (1kg), thinly sliced

2 tablespoons olive oil

60g butter

3 teaspoons thyme leaves

4 cloves garlic, crushed

1/4 cup (40g) chopped seeded black olives

1¹/₂ cups (225g) plain flour

60g butter

2 tablespoons grated parmesan cheese

125g cream cheese

1 egg

1–2 tablespoons lemon juice

150g goat cheese

PLACE ONIONS in a heatproof bowl; pour in enough boiling
water to cover. Let the onions stand for about 15 minutes; drain
well. Heat oil and butter in a large heavy-based pan. Add the
onions, cook over low heat, stirring occasionally, for about
20 minutes or until the onions are very soft and golden brown.
Stir in thyme, garlic and olives, cook for a further 10 minutes
on low. Let cool to room temperature.

LIGHTLY GREASE 23cm (9") flan tin; place the tin on an oven
tray. Process flour, butter, parmesan and half the cream cheese
until combined. Add egg and enough juice to make ingredients
cling together. Roll out dough large enough to cover base
and sides of prepared tin, lift it into tin, trim edge. Bake blind
in a moderately hot oven for 20 minutes or until pastry is crisp
and lightly golden. Let pastry shell cool.

MIX TOGETHER the remaining cream cheese and goat cheese;
spread over pastry shell. Top with onion mixture and bake in
a moderate oven for about 30 minutes or until filling is firm.
Serve at room temperature.

Serves 6 as a main or 8 as an entree.

This tart will keep well in the refrigerator for several days,
removed from tin and covered. Serve at room temperature.

asparagus

PHOTO: SCOTT CAMERON

SPRING IS SPRUNG!
ASPARAGUS BREAKS ITS COVER

Golden daffodils or sweetly perfumed freesias announce that spring is here, but keen cooks are out there watching for the first spears of asparagus to break through their richly manured beds.

Asparagus has been called both the King and Queen of vegetables. The versatility of this regal vegetable is hard to beat. It has a flavour all its own yet easily accompanies other distinctive flavours – especially fish. Purple spears are sometimes available at greengrocers. They are similar in flavour to the white and green spears and turn green when cooked.

in the garden

What do you need for a harvestable stand of asparagus? The right conditions, it seems, as they are often observed growing by roadsides or massed along canal edges, completely independent of careful farming practices.

The soil must be rich with loads of well-rotted manure (cattle grazing in the uphill paddock helps) and plenty of winter moisture (a deeply banked river edge, should you be so fortunate). But the other major requirement is a cool winter; that is, snow or frosts or day temperatures regularly below 10°C (50°F). Alas, these aren't easy to reproduce. But if the weather is against you, asparagus may still be well worth a try. The other requirement for asparagus is space; at least 1 square metre (1 square yard) or a 2m (6') row.

You can start asparagus from seed, but this adds an extra 2 years to its establishment. Most gardeners buy 2-year-old crowns, the term for the root stock. Plant in early spring 10–15cm (4–6") deep in trenches with added manure and a little lime if the soil is acid. Place at least 30cm (12") apart. Fill the trench, add slow-release fertiliser and water well. Choose a quiet, undisturbed spot as asparagus, as a perennial, can live for 20 years or more.

Don't harvest the first year's spears and only harvest lightly in the second. Asparagus plants must be well-established. To encourage the development of a strong root system over the first summer, feed and water generously through the hot months. Always leave some spears to grow into leafing stems each year, as the green is essential for root development each summer.

In autumn, the leaves will turn golden and in winter asparagus plants are pruned back to ground level. For white (blanched) asparagus, hill up old manure or compost 25–30cm (10–12") over the plants in late winter. For green spears, add a light covering of manure or compost and let the stems develop in sunlight.

PRESERVING THE CROP

STORING Wrap asparagus in a clean tea-towel in a vegetable storage bag for several days.

FREEZING Asparagus can be frozen after blanching (see Freezing, page 117). Do not thaw before using; drop in boiling water for about 2 minutes or until heated through.

To harvest, cut green spears when they are 15–20cm (6–8") long (or, if longer, where they snap) and before the tips open. To cut white spears, wait until the hilled spears break through the surface, push the knife into the soil for 15cm (6") and cut the stems off below the ground. Harvest every day for 6–8 weeks.

for the table

to prepare...

✎ Like most vegetables, asparagus spears taste better if eaten the day they are harvested. If your asparagus comes from a mature plant, the spears will be thicker. If the spears look tough, peel the outer layer from the base. Cut the base from the spears before using and, if stored for several days, snap off the ends rather than cut them. The spears will break at the point that is fresh.

✎ Asparagus is touted as being "difficult" to cook. Not at all. Don't bother to buy an expensive asparagus cooker. Instead, bring a large frying pan of water to the boil and add the prepared asparagus. The asparagus will change colour very quickly. For use in a salad, remove the spears immediately and place in a large bowl of iced water. To serve hot, continue to cook the spears until the water returns to the boil. Cooking times will vary according to the number of spears and their thickness. Never overcook asparagus; undercooked is best.

✎ Whole asparagus spears are best eaten with your fingers so that every morsel can be savoured.

to serve...

✎ For salads, use asparagus fresh or blanched. The addition of lemon juice or vinegar will change the colour of asparagus to a murky green so don't add any dressing until the last minute.

✎ It's traditional to serve fresh asparagus spears with rich, buttery sauces. You may like to add brown butter together with a scattering of roasted chopped hazelnuts or a strong mustard hollandaise to your regular repertoire.

✎ Asparagus also makes ideal finger food. Wrap strips of sliced smoked salmon around single blanched spears and serve with a lemon, tarragon cream dipping sauce – elegant and easy.

✎ Pour a very garlicky vinaigrette over still-warm asparagus and serve with grilled fish and baby potatoes. Sublime! All you need is a little crusty bread to mop up the sauce.

✎ Creamed asparagus soup can be made from pureed cooked asparagus. Serve either warm or cold and topped with crisp fried prosciutto and thin slices of garlic bread.

SNAPPING THE ENDS OFF SPEARS

A softly poached egg balanced on top of several warm asparagus spears and finished with shavings of parmesan cheese makes an easy entree or light lunch.

broad beans

PHOTO: THE DIGGER'S CLUB

Pods may look ready to pick but pinch
to check the size of the beans within.

Today, broad beans enjoy enormous culinary popularity. They're the
first beans of the season and have a delightful shape, colour and
flavour. Their brilliant green colour, revealed by peeling, is irresistible and
their robust and earthy flavour makes them a treat to serve.

For the gardening cook, a springtime crop of broad beans requires pre-
winter planning but the sound of bees in their flowers and their elegant
grey-green foliage makes broad beans one of the chief delights of the
spring kitchen garden.

in the garden

Broad beans are at their most productive in spring after surviving the cold
of winter. Plant in autumn to winter in most climates, but not when the soil
is very cold in frost-prone areas. The plants themselves do not mind frost, but
the seeds won't germinate in these conditions.

There are two varieties of broad beans: one grows 2m (6') tall and a dwarf
form reaches 1m (3'). Choose a site that enjoys winter sun, dig it over,
distribute blood and bone, and water well. Press the seeds 5cm (2") into the
soil 15–20cm (6–8") apart. Sow in rows running north–south for maximum
exposure to the sun, or in circular clusters. Shoots will appear in about
2 weeks. Water once and then, without too much bother except the
occasional watering, the bean plants will start to grow, but ever so slowly
compared with summer crops.

The plants will need support as the stems grow tall and soft and will become
top-heavy with beans in spring. Place a strong stake at each corner of your
patch or at intervals around the cluster and attach rounds of twine. Make the
first round at 30cm (12") high and another at 80cm (30") when needed.
Carefully tuck lanky stems into the enclosure.

White and black flowers appear as the weather warms and bees start to visit.
Tiny black beans with a flag of withered blossom mean your crop is under
way, about 18–20 weeks after planting.

The bean pods can be harvested while still pliable before the beans have
hardened. At this stage they can be cooked and eaten whole. Otherwise, let
the beans swell in the pods before picking. Press carefully the pods with your
fingers to assess how large the beans are.

Any beans that escape your spring harvesting will be found later, dried on
the plants. Store for use next season or, if not mouldy, store as dried beans.
An alert: some people of Mediterranean origin are allergic to broad beans.

PRESERVING THE CROP

STORING Do not remove the beans from
their pods until you are ready to cook
them. Store broad beans in the refrigerator
for up to a week.

FREEZING If blanched, without their
pods, broad beans can be frozen for
up to 6 months (see Freezing, page 117).

for the table

to prepare...

— If you pick broad beans very young, they can be eaten pods and all. But generally, the pods are harvested later and only the podded beans are eaten. Cook in plenty of boiling water, without a lid.

— Broad beans can also be cooked in the microwave. Place podded beans in a microwave-safe dish with a little water, cover and cook until tender.

to serve...

— Broad beans are traditional partners with Mediterranean flavours. They complement tomato-based lamb dishes particularly well.

— Add cooked and peeled broad beans to casseroles at the last minute; they add flavour and great colour.

— For an easy salad, combine cooked, peeled broad beans and asparagus in a herbed vinaigrette. Don't dress the salad too early as the vinaigrette discolours the green vegetables.

— Gently fry onions and garlic with tarragon. Add cooked and peeled broad beans and toss gently until heated through. Serve as a side dish.

— For a broad beans dip, cook beans well, peel and puree with a little lemon juice, sour cream, ground cumin and lots of fresh herbs. Press plastic wrap to the surface of the dip to prevent discolouring.

Broad beans must be cooked well. It's not necessary to remove the grey, outer skin after cooking, but if you do have the time and inclination you will be rewarded with the beautifully brilliant green beans.

char-grilled chicken with broad beans and chive butter

The bean mixture can also be served as a vegetarian dish over polenta or as a side dish to a main course.

750g broad beans, podded
1 tablespoon olive oil
1 small red onion (100g), thinly sliced
2 cloves garlic, crushed
2 medium tomatoes (380g), chopped
2 tablespoons chopped fresh parsley
1 tablespoon olive oil, extra
4 single chicken breast fillets (680g)
60g butter
2 tablespoons snipped fresh chives

BOIL, steam or microwave beans until tender; cool and remove the grey skin.

HEAT THE OIL in a medium frying pan and cook the onion, covered, over low heat until very soft and starting to caramelise. Add garlic and beans and stir until heated through. Stir in tomato, parsley and season with pepper and salt; stir over low heat for 5 minutes.

HEAT EXTRA OIL in a ridged grill pan. Cook chicken for 5–7 minutes, turning once until cooked through.

COMBINE BUTTER and chives in a small bowl.

SERVE CHICKEN on the bean mixture and top with chive butter.

Serves 4.

Bean mixture can be made a day ahead and gently reheated when required.

beetroot

WASHING A FRESHLY PICKED BUNCH

Beetroot makes an amazing dip. Roast without peeling, then peel, puree with a little sour cream and flavour with garlic, cumin and salt.

The traditional red beetroot is being given a run for its money by the development of different-coloured varieties. They make interesting garden experiments and offer superior flavour. Golden beetroot, which turns from orange to yellow when cooked, and the white-fleshed 'Albina Vereduna' are both particularly sweet. An Italian variety, 'Chioggia', has alternately reddish and white rings, like a red onion; and another variety, 'Cylindra' is red and cylindrical, instead of round. This is very handy because it produces evenly sized slices when cut. You may have to seek out specialist seed suppliers to find these unusual varieties.

in the garden

Beetroot grow in full sun but can survive some shade, in dappled light under a tree line or for half a day in the shadow of a fence. The soil should be prepared with decomposed manure, dug in well to break it up. Add blood and bone, pelleted poultry manure or any general fertiliser at planting time.

Seeds are knobbly clusters, like the seeds of silverbeet or Swiss chard, to which beetroot is closely related. Seeds can be planted from spring to early autumn in temperate and cool Continental climates. It is said the sweetest bulbs are those that are exposed to the first frost of winter. In Mediterranean and subtropical gardens, plant after the hottest part of summer to prevent plants bolting to seed. In the tropics you can plant all year, though the wet season is probably risky.

Push the seed in to the depth of your first knuckle every 10cm (4") and cover them over. Water regularly and the seedlings will emerge in 2 weeks. Where 2-3 seedlings have grown from the cluster seeds, separate and transplant them into new rows. Seedlings are also available from your nursery. Plant them at suggested spacings into soil prepared as above.

Regular watering will prevent the beets becoming woody, and a spray with fish food fertiliser or a complete plant food every 2 weeks will supply nitrogen and all the trace elements to aid root development.

About 10 weeks after sowing, small bulbs are ready to be gathered as baby beets. If you want larger beets, leave them longer. As the beets sit on the soil surface you can assess their size without problems. Don't hill the soil over them. It's a good idea to harvest alternate beets as you need them. Those left in the row will have more space to expand. But don't be mistaken into thinking they'll last indefinitely; that tender flesh of youth can become leathery. Follow-up crops can be planted every 4-5 weeks.

for the table

to prepare...

Handle beetroot carefully to avoid breaking the skin as this causes them to bleed. To prevent bleeding, always leave about 3cm (1 1/4") of stalk on the beetroot when storing or cooking whole.

Beetroot can also be cooked in the microwave. Pierce the skin several times and wrap the beets individually in microwave-safe wrap and cook 20–30 minutes if large. Turn halfway through cooking.

to serve...

Roasted beetroot are beautiful. Wrap individually in foil and cook with the Sunday roast. Do not peel until they are cooked.

The perfect salad vegetable, beetroot can be eaten raw, cooked or pickled. If adding to a salad, do so at the last minute as the beetroot will turn everything purple and there is nothing you can do about it.

Roasted beetroot with a Lebanese-style garlic sauce makes a great side dish to strongly flavoured meats such as venison or rabbit.

Wedges of beetroot can be cooked in butter or oil then braised in red wine and stock with peppercorns. Serve as a hot vegetable.

PRESERVING THE CROP

STORING Beetroot keeps for several days in the refrigerator. Never store leaves and bulbs together as the leaves cause the beets to shrivel and become soft.

FREEZING Cooked and peeled beetroot can be chopped or sliced and frozen for up to 6 months (see Freezing, page 117). Thaw in the refrigerator and sauté in butter or oil and herbs or serve in salads.

home-pickled beetroot

Use either caster or brown sugar and experiment with the spices to vary the flavour. You can also cook whole baby beets in this manner and the cooking time will be about 15 minutes.

6 medium beetroot (960g)
1 cup (220g) sugar
4 cups (1 litre) cider vinegar
1 small cinnamon stick
8 black peppercorns
4 small dried red chillies
1 teaspoon black mustard seeds

TRIM BEETROOT, leaving 3cm (1 1/4") of the stem attached. Wash carefully. Add to a large pan of cold water and boil for 45 minutes to 1 hour until tender. Allow to cool in the cooking water. Reserve 1/2 cup (125ml) of the liquid. Rub the skins off. Slice or quarter and place in hot sterilised jars (see Bottling, page 118). Combine reserved cooking liquid, sugar, vinegar and flavourings in a large non-corrosive pan, stir over heat, without boiling, until sugar is dissolved, then bring to the boil. Pour over beetroot and seal while hot. Store in a cool, dark place for up to 6 months.

spring herbs

POTTED HERBS READY FOR PLANTING

Throughout winter, the hardier members of the herb set will have survived to keep our food tasty and seasonal. Come spring in the garden we look for the tender perennials like tarragon and Vietnamese mint, chives re-emerge and we discover self-sown seedlings of dill, borage, basil, parsley, coriander or nasturtium popping up in appropriate and crazy places.

in the garden

parsley

Hopefully, parsley will have stayed productive through winter, in stunted form if your winter is very cool, but come the warmth of spring and longer daylight hours, the stems elongate and thicken. Parsley is a biennial plant (that is, it has a 2-year life cycle) and if you planted your parsley 2 years ago, it will probably start to seed this year.

To start new supplies, sow seeds through the warm months in punnets, pots or in the ground. Soak the seeds overnight to speed up germination.

If you let parsley go to seed, in no time you'll have tall, green, flowery tops and the many seeds will settle throughout your garden and provide you with copious new plants. It's said you have to be particularly wicked to get returns of parsley, but perhaps what should be said is that you're very lucky.

chives

Chives are small-growing, well-behaved members of the onion family. The grassy clumps stand 30cm (12") tall and have pink–mauve flowers in spring. Chives are equally happy grown in pots, garden clumps or as border plants. They like a sunny, well-drained spot but can also cope with shade.

Don't attempt to grow chives in soggy conditions. They can be grown from seed or divided from a larger clump; otherwise buy a small pot from your nursery for an instant useable addition to your garden.

The soil should be richly manured. Liquid fertiliser should be given at least every month as you are growing a leafy plant. When the tips start to yellow, you know extra nourishment is needed.

As the cool weather approaches, the leaves will die down, even in subtropical gardens. Remember to mark the spot to avoid disturbing the clump during winter gardening. In spring the chives will re-emerge. They can then be lifted and divided. This strengthens cluster bulbs.

Garlic chives have strappy leaves, longer than traditional chives and white flower clusters. The furled buds are used in Chinese stir-fries. These chives also have an excellent garlic flavour and don't scent the breath, hence their other name, "society garlic". They like the same conditions and grow in the same manner as normal chives. Wild garlic, *Tulbaghia violacea*, can be also used in the same way.

chervil

Chervil is an unusual herb because it grows happily in shade. Not deep shade but filtered sun is preferred. It is also happy in a large pot, making it very convenient for small city gardens. In both gardens and pots, chervil needs to be kept moist.

Chervil is fern-like both in its appearance and growth. In good conditions, it will grow for about 18 months before running to flower and seed. Gather some seeds and plant immediately. (If it's the middle of winter, wait until spring.) Its leaves are fine, so harvest gently with scissors to avoid pulling out the plant accidentally.

tarragon

Tarragon, or *Artemesia dracunculus*, is a tender, delicately flavoured perennial sometimes called the "King of Herbs". Seek out French tarragon in preference to Russian tarragon as the flavour is superior.

Buy a pot in spring or ask a neighbour for some newly emerging offshoots (there will be an abundance). Plant in a spot at least 1 square metre (1 square yard) in full sun in soil which has been well manured with blood and bone or a pelleted slow-release fertiliser. Water well until established. Tarragon multiplies like mint so keep your spade handy to control the spread.

coriander

This herb, essential in Asian cooking, is a parsley-like annual (often called Chinese parsley). The thing to remember is that coriander prefers to burgeon when the weather is cooler (spring, autumn and even through mild winters).

Coriander's worst characteristic is running to seed, particularly in summer when it sometimes bolts. Just when you've got a row of seedlings up, or planted out seedlings into a sunny spot, they suddenly change leaf shape to develop fern-like foliage and a flower on top. Save the seeds. They can be ground or used whole in cooking, or kept for future planting.

To avoid premature seeding, try planting during cooler conditions and adding massive doses of nitrogen to extend its growing time. Snip off leaves as required. This will thicken the plant. Pull out whole plants when bunches or roots are needed. This will thin the row or cluster and allows the remaining plants to grow more robust.

Vietnamese mint, which grows all through summer and all year in frost-free areas, is a reasonable flavour substitute for coriander.

PRESERVING THE CROP

STORING Herbs are best used straight from the garden, but can be wrapped in damp paper towel and stored in a vegetable storage bag in the refrigerator for several days. The flavour won't be as good so be generous.

FREEZING All these spring herbs can be frozen (see Freezing, page 117). Coriander roots can also be frozen.

DRYING Parsley, chervil and tarragon can all be dried successfully (see Drying, page 119) as can the flowers of chives and tarragon. Coriander loses its flavour when dried.

Store coriander seeds in an airtight container in a cool, dark, dry place.

Most herbs grow well in pots and can be handy to the kitchen, but remember to feed and water regularly.

Chervil makes an excellent potted plant with its attractive leaves. You can move it around to provide semi-shade in summer.

for the table

to serve...

∼ Toss the whole leaves of freshly harvested herbs through salads for an instant flavour boost.

∼ Roll a boned loin of pork or veal in chopped mixed spring herbs. Tarragon, chervil, parsley and chives are all good. Add some brown sugar and a few caraway seeds. Wrap tightly in plastic wrap and refrigerate overnight. Roast as normal.

∼ CHERVIL has a delicate, slightly aniseed flavour and is used fresh in salads or sprinkled over vegetables. It goes well with egg, chicken and cheese dishes. Add a handful of chervil leaves to a gruyère soufflé, for instance.

∼ TARRAGON is famous as a vinegar flavouring. Use a quality white wine vinegar and store for 1 month. New tarragon growth has the most flavour. Add fresh at the end of slow-cooked dishes as it becomes bitter if cooked.

∼ PARSLEY is full of vitamins and minerals, including iron. It aids digestion and keeps the kidneys healthy. The two varieties are virtually interchangeable but flat-leaf parsley tends to holds its flavour better and performs best in salads while curly-leaf parsley is best for garnishing. Add the stems of parsley to stocks (the leaves make the stock cloudy). Sprinkle gremolata (parsley, lemon rind and garlic) over rich casseroles such as lamb shanks and osso buco just before serving.

∼ CHIVES are delicate, so snip them with scissors, rather than chopping with a knife which will mince them. Chives add a slight onion flavour and are great in cheese and egg dishes as well as salads and dips. The flowers are edible and look beautiful in salads.

∼ CORIANDER is an incredibly useful herb because every part of the plant is edible. It is essential to many Asian dishes and its pungent aroma is magical to many. Add the chopped leaves and ground seed to guacamole. The dried seeds are used whole or ground in both sweet and savoury dishes. Add the leaves and the chopped root to stir-fries and curries. Spark up your nachos with a tomato and fresh coriander salsa.

coriander crisps

1 cup (150g) plain flour

1/4 cup (35g) self-raising flour

1 teaspoon ground coriander seeds

1 teaspoon ground cumin seeds

60g butter

1 tablespoon lemon juice

1/3 cup (80ml) water

1 egg white

1 tablespoon sea salt flakes

Process flours, seeds and butter until combined. Add juice and enough water to make ingredients cling together. Roll out dough to 3mm (1/8") thick and cut into desired shapes. Place on lightly greased oven trays. Brush with egg white and sprinkle with salt. Bake in moderately hot oven for about 10 minutes or until golden and crisp. Cool on wire racks.

These crisps are ideal for little lunches at school. They can be stored in an airtight container for up to 2 weeks.

double dips

Change the herbs according to what you like and what is available. Try adding
60g goat cheese instead of half of the cream cheese. Spread cheese mixture on
a toasted French stick and top with the tomato dip and a coriander leaf, if desired.

125g cream cheese, chopped

1/2 cup (125g) sour cream

2 cloves garlic, crushed

1 tablespoon chopped fresh parsley

1 tablespoon chopped fresh tarragon

1 tablespoon chopped fresh chervil

*1 tablespoon finely snipped
    fresh chives*

*2 medium tomatoes (380g),
    finely chopped*

1/2 small red onion (50g), finely grated

1 small fresh red chilli, finely chopped

1/2 teaspoon ground coriander seed

*1 tablespoon chopped fresh
    coriander leaves*

COMBINE CHEESE, cream, garlic, parsley,
tarragon, chervil and chives in a bowl;
mix well. Season with pepper and salt,
if desired. Cover, refrigerate for a couple
of hours; remove from refrigerator
10 minutes before serving.

COMBINE remaining ingredients in
a small bowl. Serve with coriander
crisps (see recipe opposite).

Serves 6–8.

Cheese dip can be made up to a day
ahead. Store, covered in refrigerator.
Tomato dip is best made close to serving.

Summer

PEACHES: A SIMPLE SEASONAL DELIGHT

Summer
garden diary

Summertime and the living is easy.

The heat is thick around us; it slows us down. The pace of living becomes languid, less urgent. A shady verandah invites us to sit, sip a long cool drink, to read, to sleep. We plan expeditions to the nearest watering hole. Long afternoon shadows are cast across the lawn. We come home from the beach sunburnt and tired. Mad dogs and Englishmen ... it's just too hot to do anything.

Not so in the garden. Summer gardens don't slow down; they speed up. Everything grows like mad, leaves develop, fruits ripen overnight, vines unfurl before your eyes. The garden threatens to take over. Insects and diseases multiply to take advantage of the bounty. All your careful spring preparations pay dividends as summer fruits and vegetables burgeon around you.

Water becomes scarce and your garden will almost certainly need your help to avoid drying out. Maintain a schedule of regular watering. Remember to water in the cool of the day (early morning or late afternoon) to minimise evaporation and leaf burn.

Install a watering system, especially if you are planning a long holiday. Pots, in particular, dry out very quickly so need careful and constant monitoring.

Spread mulch around beds to retain soil moisture and protect roots. Plant "thirsty" plants together to make thorough watering easier. Irrigate with furrows between plants so that water goes directly to the roots. Avoid growing those plants that you find too demanding for your cultivating conditions.

And remember to take care of yourself. Don't work in the middle of the day and always wear protection against the sun, even in the mornings and evenings. Do only the essential maintenance tasks and leave the heavy garden jobs for autumn or winter.

Most important of all, gather your harvest when it's at its peak. Enjoy the summertime treasures you and your garden have produced.

pick now...

MOST GARDENS

- artichokes
- beans
- beetroot
- cabbage
- carrots
- capsicums
- chillies
- Chinese cabbage
- cucumbers
- eggplant
- leeks
- lettuce
- potatoes
- radish
- silverbeet
- squash
- sweet corn
- tomato
- zucchini

COOL GARDENS

- broad beans

SUBTROPICAL GARDENS

- summer vegetables
- salad crops
- passionfruit

TROPICAL GARDENS

- ginger
- mangoes
- water chestnuts
- mildew-resistant vegetables grown in pots protected from the "wet"

plant now...

MOST GARDENS

- basil
- beans
- cabbage
- lettuce
- parsley
- potatoes
- silverbeet

COOL GARDENS

- coriander
- peas

SUBTROPICAL GARDENS

- corn
- cucumber
- tomatoes
- zucchini

LATE-SUMMER CROPS FOR WINTER

- Asian greens
- broccoli
- cabbage
- cauliflower
- leeks
- onions

CLOCKWISE FROM TOP LEFT A border of box holds back exuberant *Zinnia augustifolia* and basil; borlotti beans can be used whole when small and podded when large; flowers like dahlias attract bees to the garden; produce galore: strawberries, red runner beans, bush beans, a bank of corn and final sprouts of broccoli.

tomatoes

RIPENING CLUSTER OF YELLOW TOMATOES

What's a summer vegetable garden without tomatoes? The first ripe tomato of the season is a guaranteed thrill for every gardener. It will probably be only enough for a single sandwich or perhaps a salad, but it will taste like ambrosia. What flavour! What perfume!

As summer progresses, and your tomatoes swing into full production, you'll harvest armfuls each evening. And you'll have the opposite situation of what do you do with the sheer volume? Luckily, tomatoes are easy to preserve, and you'll be able to capture this rich, ripe aroma of summer.

That is, until next summer when you once again await that first tomato.

in the garden

Tomatoes need well-drained soil with plenty of manure or compost dug in before planting. They also require the complete fertiliser of your choice, be it chemical or organic, to really develop well.

Tomatoes generally require full sun, but in hot climates with daily temperatures over 35°C (95°F) the fruit can get sunburnt without some shade after midday. Tomatoes cannot stand frost.

Nursersies sell seedlings, and grafted plants are available with disease-resistant rootstock. You can also buy seeds to raise in pots or trays in warm, frost-free gardens or under glass or house protection in cold zones while frosts continue and the soil is cold. Seedlings take about 6 weeks to mature to transplantable size. If they develop too fast and the conditions aren't yet right, move the seedlings to 15–20cm (6–8") pots until the garden is ready.

'Grosse Lisse', 'Rouge de Marmonde' and 'Mortgage Lifter' are among the popular, large-fruiting types. Egg-shaped tomatoes like 'Roma' are traditionally grown for preserving, drying and sauce-making as they are fleshy rather than juicy. There are assorted streaked and mottled tomato varieties, too.

The other main tomato variety is the small fruiters producing grape-like clusters in a range of shapes and colours. Some, such as 'Tommy Toe', are slightly bigger than bite-sized; others such as 'Tiny Tim' are cherry-sized. These usually show more resistance to fruit-fly and are the best for growing in pots. They will need a rich potting mix and regular watering.

You'll also find that many volunteer seedlings will appear from last season's dropped fruit or compost. Transplant them if needed but remove them if you want to concentrate on specific varieties.

Plant your seedlings in a prepared sunny position. Space them about 1m (3') apart but if space is limited, they can be spaced at 50-60cm (20-24") intervals when staked. Hammer in strong stakes at planting time to avoid disturbing the roots later. Close planting requires regular watering and fertilising. Tomatoes develop large root systems, so give them as much space as you can.

Make furrows between the plants so the roots can be easily soaked. Avoid overhead hosing as it encourages leaf viruses and diseases. A good soaking every couple of days will keep your tomatoes growing well.

Plants can be let to ramble naturally (they have a wide spread) or controlled on stakes by removing the side growths (from leaf axils) when they are about 3cm (1") long. These can be planted in pots or in another part of the garden for a second crop. Don't remove the differently shaped flower spikes (you'll see the buds). Keep tying the plants to the stakes in loose figure-of-eight ties and break off the tip to halt growth when it reaches the top of the stake.

The flower stems will start to appear in 6-12 weeks and the fruit will form if there is good air movement to distribute the pollen and night temperatures are over 10°C (50°F). The tastiest fruit are those that ripen on the plant.

Tomatoes can be grown under glass if conditions are too cool, but buy appropriate varieties and make sure there is good ventilation.

pests and diseases

If fruit-fly is a problem, use proprietary chemical sprays or sweet wine traps. Some gardeners wrap paper bags around the ripening fruit. Harvesting tomatoes early while still green can also reduce fruit-fly strike.

Pyrethrum-based sprays are a safe treatment for thrips, white fly and tomato caterpillar. There are also proprietary chemical treatments for the many fungal blights that tomatoes are heir to, but Bordeaux spray may be an

CHERRY TOMATOES

TEARDROP TOMATOES

VINE-RIPENED TOMATOES

ROMA TOMATOES

alternative. Drop any infected or diseased fruit in hot water, burn it or seal in plastic bags to bake in the sun. Don't compost any fruit infected by fungal blights as the spores don't die in the process.

Lastly, don't be put off by these dire warnings. Most gardeners raise terrific crops, and most tomato plants produce something, even in dire straits.

for the table

to prepare...

For the best taste, leave tomatoes on the vine for as long as possible to allow their flavour to fully develop. When picked, store at room temperature. They will be much sweeter than those stored in the refrigerator as cold dulls their flavour. Tomatoes can last up to a week at room temperature in hot weather and 3–4 weeks in the refrigerator.

to serve...

Serve freshly sliced tomatoes, with a scattering of shredded fresh mint, ground black pepper and a drizzle of olive oil, as an accompaniment to easy summer dinners such as grilled fish, barbecued meats or chicken.

Cherry tomatoes wrapped in long thin slices of Lebanese cucumber, secured with a toothpick and served with pesto-flavoured mayonnaise make great summer finger food.

For a quick lunch, toss halved teardrop and cherry tomatoes in a vinaigrette dressing. Serve on warm damper with fresh rocket and some strong cheddar cheese.

A tip for school lunches – for non-soggy sandwiches, hold the tomato with the stem end up and slice through it to the base, not across the tomato.

DRYING TOMATOES

There are two methods: oven-drying and sun-drying. For either method, 'Roma' or egg tomatoes, and cherry tomatoes have less juice and are therefore easier (see also Drying, page 119).

Good sun and low moisture are needed for sun-drying. Place halved tomatoes cut-side up on wire racks in a deep baking dish and place in the sunniest possible position. Dry fresh thyme or oregano at the same time to add as extra flavour when bottling. Drying should take 3–4 days, the fruit becoming darker the longer it is dried. Bring indoors each night to avoid dew.

Oven-drying is faster. Prepare tomatoes on racks in oven trays, as above. Scatter thinly sliced cloves of garlic and oregano sprigs over the top. Cook in a very slow oven for about 30 minutes, remove the oregano if completely dry, continue cooking for another hour, then remove the garlic if crisp and dry. Reserve both herbs and garlic. Continue cooking for a total of about 8 hours (5 hours for cherry tomatoes) or until they are quite dry (turn them several times while drying).

Pack into hot sterilised jars (see Bottling, page 118), adding the dried garlic and oregano; completely cover with warmed, good-quality olive oil. Leave about 1cm (¹/₂") between the lid and the top of the oil. Store in a dark, cool, dry place for up to 8 months. Drain tomatoes before using, but keep the oil for cooking as it will add a boost of tomato flavour.

Semi oven-dried tomatoes are cooked for 2 hours only. They are delicious tossed through salads with olives and balsamic vinegar. They have a much shorter shelf-life – about 5 days if stored covered and in a little olive oil, in the refrigerator.

PHOTO: SCOTT CAMERON

POURING OIL OVER SUN-DRIED TOMATOES

really useful sauce

This recipe is one of the most useful you will ever try. The sauce can be frozen and then, when needed, added to recipes when you are just too busy to start from scratch. Add it to mince for instant Bolognaise sauce, or serve straight over pasta. Spoon a little over grilled chicken or steak. The sauce can also be cooked a little longer to make it thick enough to serve on garlic croutons. It can also be heated and thinned with a little tomato juice and a dash of sherry to make a great soup served topped with shaved parmesan and grilled sour dough bread.

1/3 cup (80ml) olive oil

4 small onions (320g), finely chopped

20 medium tomatoes (3.8kg)

8 cloves garlic, crushed

2/3 cup chopped fresh basil leaves

salt and pepper to taste

HEAT THE OIL in large pan, add onions, cover and cook over low heat for 20 minutes, stirring occasionally.

MEANWHILE peel, seed and chop the tomatoes, discarding stem ends.

ADD THE GARLIC to the pan and cook, stirring occasionally, for 5 minutes. Add the tomatoes. Bring to the boil, reduce the heat and simmer, uncovered, for about 1 1/2 hours or until the mixture is the consistency of a pasta sauce. Stir in basil. Continue cooking, stirring occasionally, for 10 minutes then season to taste with salt and pepper. Pour sauce into freezer containers leaving 1–2cm (1/2–1") space above the sauce for expansion. Cover, cool in the refrigerator, then freeze for up to 6 months or store in the refrigerator where it will last for up to 5 days.

Makes about 2.5 litres (10 cups).

PRESERVING THE CROP

The vine-ripened summer sweetness of tomatoes is easily captured for the cold months ahead.

STORING Tomatoes are best stored at room temperature for up to a week. They can also be stored in the refrigerator for 3–4 weeks.

FREEZING Tomatoes can be frozen, but they won't hold their shape when thawed, making them useful only in cooked dishes. The best way to freeze tomatoes is to peel, seed, chop and pack the pulp into small containers (see Freezing, page 117). Stir in chopped fresh basil for dishes that call for fresh herbs. Freeze for 6–8 months.

DRYING See drying advice, opposite page, and also Drying, page 119.

beans

Leave beans to dry on the vine for next year's seed.

Come summer the good vegetable garden is full of beans, in both senses. The garden comes alive with summertime produce and among the easiest to grow and most delightful of all garden crops is the bean family. Beans come in all shapes, colours and sizes; they grow anywhere in the sun; are perfect in small spaces and, best of all, are great to eat.

in the garden

Beans need well-manured and lightly limed soils and a frost-free summer. Plant seeds when the soil has warmed up and frosts have finished. Add a complete garden fertiliser. Beans also need sun and protection from wind.

Push seeds down to your second knuckle, or make a 3cm (1¼") deep furrow and drop them in 10–15cm (4–6") apart. Cover and they will emerge in about a week. A layer of compost, lucerne hay or leaf mulch will protect the roots, maintain soil moisture and suppress weeds. Beans require regular watering once the pods start to develop or they'll grow misshapen and stained.

Pick regularly when the pods are thin and the beans are tiny or fully formed. Detach the pods gently, preferably with scissors, to avoid snapping the stems. Should you miss some and the pods become wavy with enlarged seeds, pick and shell them and cook the seeds fresh. They take about 20 minutes to soften and can be served on their own, added to sauces or served with whole beans.

After about 2 months the leaves will crinkle, lose colour and drop off. Cut off stems 10cm (4") above the soil and add all stem and leaf matter to the compost. Collect missed dried bean pods for next season's planting. Dig in the roots as they contain nitrogen.

You can also leave beans to dry on the vine until straw-coloured. Finish drying them under cover, then pod and store in an airtight container. While most bean varieties have white seeds, borlotti develop white and pink-streaked seeds, purple beans have pale green seeds and many climbers have brown seeds. Dried beans need to be soaked before cooking.

annual beans

These are planted each spring. They grow, flower and fruit through summer and die down when the weather cools. Climbers will happily twist their way 2–3 metres (7–10') skyward over fences and walls, around lattice, stakes, tripods, netting, even wander up and over tall flowers and shrubs. Tripods can also be used in large pots if space is limited. Dwarf beans grow to 50cm (20") tall. They form bushes, don't require support, and are good as borders. They are, however, not as productive as the climbing varieties.

PRESERVING THE CROP

STORING Beans are best picked as close to serving as possible. They can be stored in the refrigerator for a day or so, but never in plastic as they go mouldy rapidly.

FREEZING All beans are suitable to freeze for up to 6 months. Blanch before freezing (see Freezing, page 117). Cook borlotti beans before freezing. Do not thaw beans before use. If adding to cooked dishes, add in the final stages.

runner beans

These are perennial beans and are good to grow where summers are cool. Their other name is "seven-year beans" as they reshoot in spring for a number of years. They won't form pods if the summer is too hot. Pick the pods when only 15cm (6") long and before the seeds have swollen. If left on the vine, they become tough and the plant doesn't produce extra flowers and beans.

Both annual and runner beans come in all shapes, sizes and colours. Purple or yellow-podded types are available as well as red-, purple- or pink-flowered forms. Some pods are flat and others are rounded; some have strings and others are stringless; some are short at about 12cm (5") long while others, such as snake beans, reach 50cm (20"). The beans within can be the usual green, yellow, purple or streaked with red.

pests and diseases

White flies are a common pest. They suck the plant juices and weaken them, and can be seen hovering when the leaves are disturbed. Spray with insecticide or use one of the alternative treatments given on page 9.

Leaf abnormalities include halo blight (halo spots on pale leaves) which is death to the plant (burn or seal leaves in plastic bags to dispose), and rust spots and powdery mildew, both of which can be treated with proprietary sprays or baking soda spray (see page 9).

FRESH BORLOTTI BEANS

for the table

to prepare...

~ Cook all fresh beans in boiling water, uncovered, for about 5 minutes or until just tender. (Purple beans turn green when cooked). For salads, remove early and cool in iced water.

~ Microwave beans in a microwave-safe dish with a tablespoon of water, for 3–5 minutes on HIGH.

~ Children enjoy snacking on beans fresh from the garden. Asking them to pick the beans can be a way of making sure they eat their greens!

to serve...

~ Toasted nuts make the perfect accompaniment to any bean. Toss beans in a little brown butter and add a sprinkling of nuts.

~ Try beans with chopped basil and garlic with a squeeze of lemon juice added at the last minute as lemon juice will discolour the beans.

~ Combine beans with a tarragon-flavoured vinaigrette and serve warm or at room temperature.

~ Borlotti beans and tomatoes seem to be made for each other. Simmer them in Really Useful Sauce (see page 39) for a great vegetarian treat. Pan-fried pancetta can be added for meat-eaters.

SCARLET RUNNER BEANS CLIMBING UP WIRE

cucumber

PICK CUCUMBERS WHILE STILL YOUNG

PRESERVING THE CROP

STORING Don't wash cucumbers until ready to use. Store in the refrigerator in a vegetable storage bag for about 10 days. Once cut, wrap in plastic wrap and refrigerate for up to 5 days.

FREEZING Due to their high water content, cucumbers are not suitable to freeze.

PICKLING Make pickles from young cucumbers by slicing or cutting into quarters lengthways. Toss in a little salt and stand in a colander, cover, and place over a sink or bowl, for 24 hours. Rinse thoroughly and pack into hot sterilised jars (see Bottling, page 118), pour over spiced vinegar (mustard seeds or dill seeds are good, with garlic and a few bay leaves) combined with a little sugar. Seal while hot and store in a cool, dark, dry place for 3 weeks before opening. These pickles keep for up to a year.

Cucumbers belong to a large extended family, the cucurbits, which includes the warm-season wanderers: cucumbers, squash, zucchinis (or courgettes), marrows, pumpkins and melons. Like any worthwhile gathering of relatives, the family also includes some diverting members such as loofahs for the bath and gourds for decoration.

in the garden

Cucumbers are a true summer crop: they demand full sun and are killed by frosts. They also demand soil rich in organic matter (manure, compost, decomposed leaf litter). The more, the better. Add lime or dolomite to reduce acidity and a complete garden fertiliser. In mild zones, two crops are possible by planting in both late winter and mid-to-late summer.

Shape the soil into mounds 50cm (20") apart, creating a furrow around each to allow water to reach the roots easily. Push 3–4 seeds into the mounds just below the surface. For bush or compact varieties, halve this distance or plant them in pots 30–50cm (12–20") wide and deep and packed with a rich potting mix.

Seedlings will break through in a week or so, depending on the temperature of the soil. Reduce to the healthiest 2 plants per mound once the leaves have started to form. Turn the vines to grow in opposite directions. If growing indoors, grow pairs of seedlings in egg cartons or grow-pots so they can be planted later directly into the soil without disturbing the roots.

To save space, train cucumber vines up wire, netting, lattice or tripods where their tendrils support them. Another space-saving technique is to cut off the stem after several fruit have formed. Side shoots will form and flower.

Keep cucumbers very well watered while flowering and fruiting. Each plant carries both male and female flowers. Male flowers have a prominent pollen-laden stamen in the centre. Female flowers carry an embryo fruit behind each trumpet and the flower centre is rounded. In summer there are more male flowers than female; in spring and autumn there's an equality of sexes. Bees carry the pollen between the flowers, but if bees are in short supply, brush the pollen from a male flower onto several female flowers.

Cucumbers are best picked when small when their skins are soft and the flesh is juicy. Pick early and often and more fruit will be produced.

Cucumber varieties are many and various. Elongated green cucumbers are perhaps the most commonly grown. But also available are the tiny pickling or gherkin types, the smooth-skinned Lebanese variety, ridged

'Burpee' cucumbers (10–20cm or 4–5") and the long 'Telegraph' and 'Burpless' (50cm or 20") varieties. There's a green and white striped Chinese giant that reaches 1m (3') as well as round cucumber varieties such as the white-skinned apple or 'Crystal' types. West Indian gherkin has hooks all over its pale green skin.

LEBANESE CUCUMBER

pests and diseases

Cucumbers can be stricken by downy mildew that discolours and eventually kills the leaves. It usually appears at the end of summer and signals the end of the productive season. Proprietary sprays are available and alternative treatments (see page 9) can be used. Do not compost the diseased leaves but burn or wrap them up before putting into the garbage.

Damping off is a condition where the stems of seedlings rot and the plants topple over. To combat it, do not plant the seedlings too deeply, make sure all organic matter is well rotted and don't overwater in the early stages.

Leaves are often skeletonised by the larvae of the 28-spotted orange and black ladybird that grazes on the under-surface. These ladybirds are greenish-yellow with black spines and just over 0.5cm (1/4") long. Crush them by hand or use a food-safe spray if there are fruit and bees about.

GREEN CUCUMBER

for the table

to prepare...

↬ There's no need to peel cucumbers if they are picked young. If left longer, you can either peel them or run the tines of a fork along their length, breaking the skin as you go.

↬ To crisp ageing cucumbers, cut into thick slices, sprinkle with salt, place in a colander over a sink or large bowl; add some ice-cubes and cover. Stand for about an hour; rinse thoroughly in cold water and pat dry.

To serve

↬ Sauté in butter and add a sprinkle of green onions or chives.

↬ Make a warm or cold soup from pureed cucumber, well-flavoured chicken stock and a little cream. Add dill to garnish.

↬ Cucumber cups filled with prawns in a Thai peanut sauce are a refreshing starter. Or wrap smoked ocean trout or salmon around cucumber sticks with a thin spread of wasabi for Japanese-style finger food.

↬ Finely sliced cucumber tossed with mirin, chopped fresh dill and some horseradish cream makes a wonderful bed for char-grilled fish steaks.

↬ Make fresh Vietnamese spring rolls from matchstick-thin slices of cucumber, daikon, red capsicum and carrots. Combine with soaked rice noodles and snow pea sprouts and wrap in rice paper rounds. Serve with a light soy and sesame oil dipping sauce. You can add grilled chicken, fresh prawns or chunks of rare roast beef if desired.

TELEGRAPH CUCUMBER

salad greens & edible flowers

AN ABUNDANT GREEN SALAD CROP

'ICEBERG' LETTUCE

PHOTOS: AWW HOME LIBRARY

Not any more does a salad consist of a lettuce leaf and a slice of tomato. Not any more is a salad the forgotten side dish. Today's salads are sophisticated combinations of leaf, colour, flower, shape and texture. Add an exotic dressing and tasty treats are yours – in both summer and winter.

Delicious to eat, salad greens make glorious decorative additions to the cook's garden. Grow them in pots, as borders and edges, or among the flower beds. A bed of lettuce makes an excellent winter crop in subtropical and tropical gardens but their delicate leaves won't survive frosts.

Be warned: in very warm conditions lettuce can run to seed easily and produce bitter leaves. To prevent this, select varieties that can cope with warm weather. Your local nursery will be able to advise.

in the garden

Lettuces must grow fast. They need rich, well-prepared soil. Spread 10cm (4") layer of chicken manure over a sunny, well-drained site a month before planting and cover with another layer of leaf, mushroom or well-matured garden compost. Dig all this into the soil at the end of the month.

Sprinkle seeds finely over the surface and rough up the soil to distribute. If planting in a seedling tray, cover with 0.5cm ($^1/_4$") of seed-raising mixture or sand. Water lightly and the seeds will sprout in a week or less. Lettuce seeds will not germinate when the soil is over 30°C (85°F).

Thin tray-raised seedlings to 20–30cm (8–12") apart. Transplant these or purchased seedlings into the garden at the same spacings when their true leaves form. This is best done in the cool of the day when the sun has lowered. Water lightly but thoroughly.

Mulch well to keep weeds down and protect roots, but leave the stems clear to prevent fungal stem rot. Lettuce needs regular watering and nitrogen-rich liquid fertiliser every 2 weeks. Lettuce can be grown in a heated glasshouse during winter in frosty zones.

hearting lettuce

These lettuces are the most familiar of all the salad lettuces. They grow slowly and produce large leaves that curl inwards and enwrap each other to form a central ball. The leaves are light green and crisp and remain cup-shaped when removed from their embrace, making them useful as containers in dishes such as sang choy bow. They also tear apart easily.

'Great Lakes' and 'Iceberg' are two hearting lettuces that won't bolt in warm weather. Butterheads are softer and looser. Harvest leaf by leaf until the heart has fully formed, then harvest it whole. 'Cos' or 'Romaine' varieties grow tall and have tapering oval leaves that form a loose heart. These keep better than most in the fridge and are essential for Caesar salads.

loose-leaf lettuce

With these lettuces we see the full range of colour and texture possibilities, such as the softly frilled 'Salad Bowl' and the much-divided 'Oak Leaf', the tightly frilled 'Coral' or 'Lollo' and the neatly packed 'Mignonette' varieties. All are available in green or bronze-pink tones. There is also a red-leafed 'Cos' and a yellow-leafed variety named 'Australian Yellow Leaf'.

salad greens

These are the more strongly flavoured leafy salad greens that enjoy the same growing conditions as the better-known lettuces but are in less demand. They are easy to grow in any garden as they take up little space, are ready to harvest in no time and are fun to experiment with.

ROCKET, also known as arugula, has a rich, peppery flavour. The leaves develop from the centre and are divided like dandelion leaves but have round edges. The surface is smooth and glossy. Rocket is easy to grow from seeds sown 10cm (4") apart. Cluster planting in a pot or garden is also useful, with further plantings each month. Avoid planting during the hottest months as rocket now earns its name and runs straight to seed. The leaves can be harvested leaf by leaf within a month. The plants will continue to thicken as long as they're well watered and fed. Pick off flower stems to stop early flowering but when replacements are growing, let a couple of plants bloom prettily, as they do, and collect the seeds for future plantings. With luck you'll find self-seeded volunteers all over the garden.

MIZUNA, like rocket, prefers cooler conditions for generous leafy growth. The leaves are heavily dissected and almost fern-like in appearance and the pointed tips are soft. Its flavour is not as strong as rocket but it does have its own almost grass-like taste. Leaves can be gathered in 20–30 days.

RADICCHIO comes in two guises. It can be lanky, loose-leafed and green with splashes of red or tightly furled resembling a red cabbage. Both varieties have an almost bitter flavour. Radicchio combines well with other flavours but is often preferred on its own. Most green varieties re-sprout when cut 2.5cm (1") above the ground and develop into the red-hearted form in cool weather. Always keep radicchio well watered and fed.

RED 'MIGNONETTE' LETTUCE

RADICCHIO

ROCKET

MIZUNA

PRESERVING THE CROP

STORING Salad leaves and edible flowers are best picked as you need them – they keep much better in the garden. If you have to store them, wash salad leaves, not flowers, thoroughly in cold water, wrap in a damp tea-towel and keep in the refrigerator for about 5 days at the most. Vegetable storage bags and lettuce keepers will extend their refrigerator life.

FREEZING Salad leaves and edible flowers can't be frozen due to their high water content. The thawed-out sludge is of no use to anyone.

DRYING Edible flowers can be dried (see Drying, page 119) but they will lose their flavour and colour, so use instead for pot pourri or non-culinary purposes.

ENDIVE is grown in the coolest months. It, too, has a strong and sometimes bitter flavour. The more familiar loose-leafed frilly form requires regular water and mulching to prevent its roots from drying out and bitterness developing in the leaves. Gather a few leaves at a time while they are young but if you want to harvest the whole head, partially cover it with a plate or pot saucer for 3 weeks beforehand for a less bitter taste. Its blue flowers guarantee repeat crops as it self-seeds generously.

edible flowers

Edible flowers are the special province of the cook's garden. After all, one rarely buys flowers to eat, and your kitchen garden can easily yield a plentiful supply of unusual and striking blooms and petals to team with greens for an individualised and unique salad mix.

Wash all flowers very well. Dry them gently. Take care when gathering blossoms that you don't harvest concealed bees as well. Make sure you have not used any pesticide or fungicide sprays, that your neighbour's sprays have not drifted into your garden, or that pets or birds have not left their marks.

So, what's safe to eat?

CALENDULA (*Calendula officinalis*) Its peppery orange or yellow petals are eaten raw in salads, on rice or in curries.

CHRYSANTHEMUM The petals are similar to calendula and can be used similarly.

DAY LILY (*Hemerocallis* varieties) These last only a day and colours include yellow, pink, cream, mauve and bronze. Pull off their green sepals and use the blooms whole or shredded in salads, batters or as garnishes.

ELDERFLOWER (*Sambucus nigra*) The small, white flowers form on a large head in spring, and the berries ripen to black in autumn. The flowers can be used to flavour champagne or to garnish punch; the berries are used to make wine and jellies.

FRUIT BLOSSOMS (*Citrus, Malus, Prunus*) The petals of cherries, plums, peaches, apples, crab apples and all the citrus blossoms make lightly flavoured and pretty garnishes on cakes or sweet pies. Citrus flowers can also be crystallised or steeped in gin or vodka to make a citrus essence. Wash well to remove any chemical sprays and residues.

GERANIUM AND PELARGONIUM FLOWERS AND SCENTED LEAVES Both can be used as garnishes on sweet or savoury dishes. The scented leaves will release flavour when added during cooking; citrus or peppermint varieties are the most useful.

GREVILLEA FLOWERS Often honey-laden, grevillea flowers make a striking garnish and can be used to flavour ice-cream. Some leaves can cause a rash when handled so gather carefully.

HERB FLOWERS Basil, parsley, mint, marjoram, chives and the like can be added as garnishes just before serving, but not during cooking. Blue borage flowers can be crystallised or frozen in ice cubes to add a pretty touch to drinks.

HONEYSUCKLE (*Lonicera* varieties) Remove the calyx and shred the petals of the sweetly perfumed varieties for a lightly honeyed, fragrant addition to ice-cream, milk desserts or icing.

LAVENDER The flowers of any scented lavender variety can be milled into sugar, added to ice-cream, biscuits or jams.

MARIGOLDS (*Tagetes* varieties) These are the familar, strongly aromatic group of flowers with bright yellow, orange or bronze petals. Their strong flavour and colour are used like calendula (see above).

NASTURTIUMS Both the flowers and leaves are edible with a slight peppery taste and are good in salads.

ROSE Loose petals and whole flowers can be used for garnishes, crystallised or steeped in honey (for a flavoured spread) or in alcohol (for rose essence). Roses are also used to make jams, jellies and other preserves. Dark-coloured blooms hold their colour best during cooking. Beware of bought roses as they are likely to have been sprayed with pesticides and other chemicals.

IMPORTANT NOTE

Some common plants are poisonous so don't experiment or eat anything that you are unsure about. Exclude all flowers from the *Solanaceae* family of vegetables (potatoes, tomatoes, chillies, eggplant and capsicum). All are suspect.

SPACE-SAVING TECHNIQUE

Where space is limited, harvest lettuce leaf by leaf for small supplies or plant seedlings densely (about 10cm or 4" apart in clusters or rows) and let develop to harvest a complete lettuce. Lettuce is ready to pick after 4–6 weeks. Cut off leaving a 2cm (1") stump. The stems will sprout again. Make successive sowings every 3–4 weeks of all your chosen varieties in this packed manner and you'll be "lettuced" right through.

PHOTO: VNU/LIBELLE

Bearing gifts from the garden. Salads are a great introduction to the garden and kitchen.

VEGETABLE FLOWERS The blooms of peas, beans and seeding lettuce varieties can be added to salads. Male zucchini and pumpkin flowers need to have their bitter stamen removed. They can be stuffed, then battered and fried. They can also be spread as a garnish on a quiche or frittata before baking.

VIOLET, VIOLA AND PANSY FLOWERS Their velvet petals and deep colours look beautiful when crystallised and also look good in salads.

for the table

to prepare...

~ At the risk of being repetitive, it is important to remember to pick edible flowers carefully, wash thoroughly and to make certain that no chemical sprays have been used.

to serve...

~ The centres of firm, big-hearted LETTUCE can simply be quartered and drizzled with blue cheese dressing.

~ The French make a light and tasty soup from shredded LETTUCE simmered in chicken stock with a little rice.

~ MIZUNA is elegant mixed with pear slices and enoki mushrooms, and drizzled with hazelnut oil vinaigrette. Sprinkle with chopped toasted hazelnuts.

~ Try crisp prosciutto, teardrop tomatoes, prawns and ROCKET tossed in a spicy lime dressing.

~ Add torn ROCKET leaves to pasta and toss with a chilli-tomato sauce.

~ Chicken pieces marinated in red curry paste then grilled or barbecued are great served with MIXED SALAD LEAVES, including mint. Add a squeeze of lime juice to finish.

~ Mix soft LETTUCE leaves with ROCKET and a few peach slices. Serve with a berry vinaigrette.

~ Halve RADICCHIO heads, place in an ovenproof dish, add a slurp of olive oil and season with sea salt and cracked black pepper. Cook in a hot oven for 20 minutes, turning halfway through cooking. Serve hot or at room temperature with grilled meats.

~ Make a bitter salad from shredded witlof, RADICCHIO and radish; dress with an orange vinaigrette and serve with roasted meats such as pork or duck.

~ Puree a mango with basil, lemon juice and olive oil. Use as a dressing over curly ENDIVE with edible yellow flower petals such as MARIGOLDS.

~ Edible flowers, such as ROSE PETALS and VIOLETS, can be painted with beaten egg white and dipped in caster sugar for beautiful dessert decorations.

~ Serve COS LETTUCE with a lemon pepper vinaigrette; add hard boiled eggs and shavings of parmesan cheese.

sooke harbour house flower salad

This enticing salad comes from Sooke Harbour House on Vancouver Island where the restaurant is set within a beautiful garden, all of which is edible.

Experiment with a variety of seasonal flowers and greens. Mix mild greens with a garnish of stronger-tasting flowers and vice versa. Suggested flowers include violas, calendula, culinary herb flowers, pineapple sage, dianthus, day lilies and roses. If the flowers are large, use only their petals.

250g mixed lettuce leaves

¹/₂ cup edible flowers or petals

salt and pepper to taste

RASPBERRY VINAIGRETTE

¹/₄ cup (60ml) raspberry vinegar

³/₄ cup (180ml) light vegetable oil

TOSS RINSED AND DRIED LEAVES and flowers in a salad bowl. Drizzle with raspberry viniagrette and season with salt and pepper, if desired.

RASPBERRY VINAIGRETTE Whisk together raspberry vinegar and vegetable oil; season with salt and pepper to taste.

The beautifully sited Sooke Harbour House on Vancouver Island in Canada is a restaurant that strives to grow much of what is served to guests. The garden in summer is both easy on the eye and the palate.

capsicum

HARVEST OF COLOURFUL CAPSICUM

Throughout the world these vegetables are known by a variety of names. We refer here to the sweet or mild peppers that have a fleshy skin and make a crisp crack when first cut. Their strong flavour and sweetness becomes more pronounced when cooked. Some have a mild, peppery bite and others a touch of spiciness. If you want to avoid any heat whatsoever, choose capsicum with thick skin but always check first by tasting a finger-dip of the juice.

Capsicum shapes vary. Some capsicum are long balloons, others large or narrow, tapering cones and some are small, apple-sized balls. Colours include yellow, gold, orange, green, red or purple-black, depending on the variety and their ripeness. All capsicum start life green.

in the garden

Capsicum demand similar growing conditions to tomatoes; that is, a frost-free, well-drained, well-watered, sunny site with deeply dug soil that has been well supplied with a complete fertiliser. Capsicum also like the addition of lime or dolomite to lower the soil's acidity.

Seedlings can be started indoors if there's any threat of late-winter frosts. The seeds will germinate in 2–3 weeks. Mixed-seed packets are available so you can experiment with different-coloured fruits. You can also buy seedling punnets from nurseries and share your excess with friends. Plant 50cm (20") apart and mulch well between the plants but not against their stems. Capsicum also grow well in large pots. In tropical and mild subtropical gardens, last-year's plants may have survived as scrawny shrubs. Give them a tidying prune as the weather warms and apply a complete plant food to kick-start them again.

As the plants grow, the stems thicken and the leaves conceal most of the creamy-white blossoms. Later the first fruits will become visible, drooping below the leaves. Heavily laden plants will need stakes to keep them upright.

Harvest the fruit as you need them but remember that early fruits will not be as sweet as those that reach maturity in 3–4 months after planting. While conditions remain warm, capsicum will continue to flower but be prepared to lose the last remaining fruits if frosts strike.

pests and diseases

Capsicum are subject to fruit-fly attack which can ruin a crop so use a proprietary spray or a non-chemical alternatives (see page 9). Always destroy the infected fruit and don't let it rot into the soil where the maggots pupate.

PRESERVING THE CROP

STORING Store whole capsicum in a vegetable storage bag in the refrigerator for 1^1/$_2$ to 2 weeks. Cut capsicum can be stored uncovered but it doesn't last more than a few days before becoming slimy.

Roasted, peeled capsicum can be stored in a little olive oil in the refrigerator for up to 1 week.

FREEZING Capsicum have a high water content and don't survive the freezing and thawing process at all.

for the table

to prepare...

Capsicum adds brilliant colour and an interesting sweet flavour to many dishes. Raw capsicum has a crisp, juicy texture and a fresh taste. This is quite different to the flavour and texture of capsicums after they have been roasted, cooled in plastic and peeled.

To peel capsicum, cut into quarters and remove the seeds and core. Place skin-side up under a hot grill or in a hot oven and cook until skin is black and blistered; transfer to a plastic bag until cool. Peel away the skin. If a less smoky flavour is required, rinse the pieces.

Removing the blackened and blistered capsicum pieces from the grill

to serve...

Capsicum can be used fresh in salads, sauteed or stir-fried, and they can be halved, hollowed out and stuffed. They're also good grilled on kebabs or seared, peeled and stored in olive oil. Capsicum is a must in the traditional ratatouille and, if roasted and peeled, capsicum pieces are terrific added as a colourful layer in a vegetable lasagne.

Stuff capsicum with a mixture of rice, tomatoes and tuna. Roast until the capsicum are tender and serve with a tiny dollop of pesto.

Garnish salads with a fine, jewel-like scattering of finely diced red, green and yellow capsicum.

Puree peeled red capsicum with oregano, olive oil and lots of roasted garlic and use as a dip or serve over sauteed chicken, fish or beef.

Make a warm salad of red and green capsicum roasted with garlic. A small amount of balsamic vinegar added at the end of roasting is about all you need.

For a refreshing starter, mix shredded red, green, purple and yellow capsicum and daikon, and add a dressing of chilli and coriander. Serve on top of rocket leaves with crisped lavash bread.

Combine capsicum with apples to make chutney. Flavour with peppercorns and coriander seeds. Make sure you use cider vinegar to bring out the apple flavour.

A roasted capsicum and tomato sauce is excellent served over pasta or as a sauce for roasted meats. It can also be used as a dressing for a roasted vegetable salad.

Slice capsicum and stir-fry with snow peas, baby corn and green onions; add some ginger and rice vinegar. Serve over steamed fish.

Top a pizza base with slow-fried onions and tomatoes. Add roasted and peeled capsicum strips. Use a mixture of colours, if desired. Sprinkle with crumbled goat cheese and dot with olive paste. Bake in a very hot oven and serve with a rocket and parmesan salad.

Peeling away the capsicum skin after cooling the pieces in a plastic bag

eggplant

EGGPLANTS CAN WEIGH DOWN THE BUSH

Known also as aubergine, eggplant is another member of the tomato family. It has grey, downy leaves and stems, mauve flowers and the fruit are either bulbous and egg-shaped, thin and finger-like or tiny, round balls. They may be dark, shiny purple, white, streaked with purple and white or even green, depending on the variety.

Eggplant is an interesting but slow summer cropper in the garden. It is also the great sponge of the culinary world. Eggplant readily absorbs flavours as well as vast quantities of oil.

in the garden

Eggplant grows in similar conditions to tomatoes. However, it takes a minimum of 3–4 months for the fruit to ripen and the plants will die at the first touch of a frost. For fruit to form, eggplants require night temperatures of 20°C (68°F). This can be engineered in cool zones by planting them against a protective, sun-baked wall.

Allow 8 weeks to raise seedlings ready for transplanting. Seedlings are also available from nurseries. Plant them 60–75cm (24–30") apart in warm, well-prepared soil in a sunny site where water is able to drain away quickly. Protect seedlings from late frosts with mulch or plastic wraps. Eggplant does not need as much water as tomatoes and capsicum, so a deep soaking once a week will suffice. Watch the growing tips for signs of wilting which indicates they need extra water.

Once 5 large fruits (or 5 clusters on smaller varieties) have developed, remove any extra flowers as this is all the fruit the plant can carry.

Harvest the eggplants when the skin is still shiny and yields to finger pressure. The riper the fruit, the less bitter their taste.

In tropical and mild subtropical gardens, the plants live through winter to produce again next year but prune them in autumn or early spring to generate new growth. Also give them a boost of extra fertiliser and a protective mulch. Plant new vigorous seedlings the following year.

for the table

to prepare...

Treat all types of eggplants the same. They are generally interchangeable in most recipes. Choose their shape and size according to their final appearance in the dish.

PRESERVING THE CROP

STORING Store in a cool, dry place for a couple of days but if you intend to keep eggplant longer, store in the crisper section of the refrigerator.

FREEZING Eggplant can be sliced or chopped, blanched and cooled, and then frozen for up to 8 months (see Freezing, page 117). Use in casseroles and baked dishes on thawing.

PICKLING Finger eggplants can be blanched in brine, drained and packed into hot sterilised jars (see Bottling, page 118). Pour spiced vinegar over them with a little sugar; add some chillies and sprigs of dill to enhance the flavour. Store in a cool, dark, dry place for at least 3 weeks before opening. They can be kept for up to a year. Refrigerate after opening.

⌒ The larger and older (slightly wrinkly) eggplants benefit from salting, weighting and standing, known as degorging. This is not required for finger eggplants or tiny pea eggplants.

to serve...

⌒ Roast an eggplant in a moderate oven for about 1 hour; leave to cool. The skin will be easy to remove and the flesh will have a slightly smoky flavour. Puree with flavourings, oil and lemon juice and you have the perfect dip. It can also be used as a sauce for thick-fleshed fish, such as tuna.

⌒ Make eggplant chips. Slice finely and pat the eggplant dry before frying. This helps prevent the oil splattering fiercely.

⌒ Char-grill eggplant slices and serve tossed with rocket leaves and drizzled with tarragon vinegar and a sprinkling of mint or basil.

⌒ Top Turkish bread with slices of fried eggplant, olives and parmesan cheese. Pop in a hot oven for about 15 minutes or until hot and you have a great substitute pizza.

⌒ Thick char-grilled eggplant slices can be used as a base for lamb steaks or even in place of the bun in a lamb burger.

LARGE EGGPLANTS REQUIRE DEGORGING

eggplant spread

1 large eggplant (500g), peeled, chopped
2 tablespoons vegetable oil
1 clove garlic, crushed
1/4 cup (70g) tahini
2 tablespoons lemon juice
1/4 teaspoon paprika

TO DEGORGE EGGPLANT, place in strainer, sprinkle with salt; stand 20 minutes. Rinse eggplant under cold water; drain on absorbent paper.

HEAT OIL in medium pan; cook eggplant and garlic, stirring, over low heat about 10 minutes or until eggplant is tender.

BLEND or process eggplant mixture, tahini and juice until smooth.

TRANSFER mixture to serving dish; sprinkle with paprika. Serve with crisp fresh vegetables and warm pitta bread.

Serves 4.

Can be made two days ahead; keep, covered, in refrigerator.

PHOTO: AWW HOME LIBRARY

zucchini

& squash

ZUCCHINI LEAVES ARE AS HANDSOME
AS THEIR FRUIT

PRESERVING THE CROP

STORING Store zucchini and squash in the crisper drawer of the refrigerator for up to 5 days. Do not wrap in plastic as this makes them sweat and go mouldy. Wash before using, not before storing.

FREEZING Because of their high water content, zucchini and squash don't freeze well.

PICKLING Slice thinly and brown quickly in a pan with garlic and fresh herbs (parsley and mint work well). Heat some tarragon vinegar with a little salt and a few peppercorns. Place warm zucchini into hot sterilised jars (see Bottling, page 118), pour over warmed vinegar mixture. Seal immediately and store for a week before using. Great in antipasto platters.

Zucchini, courgettes to some, have the most delightful leaves: they are large, deep green and robust-looking with very attractive white mottling. They may look lush but don't grow zucchini too near your garden paths as the leaves are rough and brittle to brush against. Squash are a little more restrained in their growth habit and do not sprawl so wide. The flowers of both zucchini and squash are edible, as well as the fruit.

in the garden

Like cucumbers and other members of the cucurbit family, zucchini and squash require similar conditions: a frost-free growing time and full sun. They also demand soil rich in organic matter (manure, garden or spent mushroom compost or well-decomposed leaf litter). Add a complete fertiliser and lime or dolomite to reduce acidity.

Wait until the soil has warmed and there is no threat of frost before planting. Shape the soil into mounds and push in 3-4 seeds to just below the surface. Both zucchini and squash ramble, so plant about 1m (3') apart to allow room to spread. Seedlings will emerge in 1-2 weeks. Once leaves have formed, thin the cluster to the 2 healthiest seedlings and turn them to grow in opposite directions. They will ramble, but they are less leggy in full sun.

If established indoors, grow seedlings in egg cartons or grow-pots to plant directly into the soil when ready. They don't like their roots to be disturbed.

Keep both zucchini and squash well watered during the growing season. An irrigation soak is preferable to splashings with a hand-held hose and will reduce the possibility of mildew developing.

The flowers are bright yellow and trumpet-shaped. Each plant carries both male and female flowers. They start to appear in 6-8 weeks. Female flowers carry the embryo fruit behind each trumpet and have a rounded centre. The male flowers have only a stem behind and a prominent pollen-laden stamen in their centre.

Bees usually carry the pollen but if they're not active, brush the pollen from a male flower onto the female centre to guarantee fruit formation. When there is an excess of male flowers, they can be gathered and eaten. Plants remain productive for 2-3 months.

zucchini

Zucchini varieties come in various colours and shapes: cylinders of light green, dark green and yellow, balls of light green and dark green, and elongated straight and crooked-neck forms. Don't leave them on the vine for too long or they will become watery and their skins will harden. Pick when small when their flesh is juicy and their seeds are small. If your crop is abundant, remember that the male flowers can be eaten: remove the stamen, fill with stuffing and then batter and lightly fry.

squash

Squash vary in colour from bright green to yellow with green tops to variegated forms. All small varieties are interchangeable with zucchini in recipes.

Button squash are currently very popular and great for small gardens. Harvest when fully shaped but still small. Otherwise, their seeds and skins harden and the blossom end rots. Compact varieties are well suited to pots.

Large white or green-skinned squash are available, as is the unusual spaghetti squash which grows into a large melon with spaghetti-like stranded flesh. These larger varieties are picked when their skins harden.

pests and diseases

Like the whole cucurbit family, zucchini and squash are prey to mildew which discolours their leaves and eventually kills the whole plant. It is caused by high humidity, rainfall or excessive watering. Proprietary sprays are available and for alternative treatments, see page 9. Do not compost diseased leaves; burn or wrap and place in the garbage. Yellow-green ladybird larvae can graze on the underside of leaves and skeletonise them. Crush them by hand or use a food-safe spray if there are fruit and bees about.

for the table

to prepare...

⟶ Add both zucchini and squash to boiling water for a couple of minutes or steam until their colour is bright and they are just tender, about 5 minutes.

to serve...

⟶ Large white or green-skinned squash are always seeded, and can be sliced and steamed or stuffed with a meat mixture and baked slowly.

⟶ Cook spaghetti squash whole, then cut in half, pick out the seeds and add the spaghetti-like flesh to pasta sauces and casseroles.

⟶ Fill zucchini flowers with fetta, ricotta, basil and pine nuts, dip in a light batter and deep-fry in batches until the batter is crisp and golden.

⟶ Bake hollowed-out zucchini boats filled with minced lamb flavoured with yogurt and cumin for a healthy dinner.

char-grilled summer vegetables with herbed yogurt dressing

4 finger eggplants (240g)

2 medium zucchini (240g)

1/4 cup (60ml) olive oil

1 medium red capsicum (200g)

1 medium yellow capsicum (200g)

1 medium green capsicum (200g)

250g pumpkin

1 bunch rocket (120g)

HERBED YOGURT DRESSING

3/4 cup (210g) reduced-fat yogurt

1 tablespoon snipped fresh chives

2 tablespoons chopped fresh parsley

1 tablespoon chopped fresh mint leaves

1 clove garlic, crushed

CUT EGGPLANT, zucchini and pumpkin into 5mm (1/4") thick slices. Cut capsicum into 2cm (1") strips. Brush vegetables with oil and char-grill on a heated ridged grill pan, turning once, until just soft. Layer vegetables with rocket and serve with herbed yogurt dressing.

HERBED YOGURT DRESSING Combine all ingredients in a small bowl; refrigerate until required.

Serves 6–8 as a side dish; 4 as a main course.

rhubarb

What a marvellous, old-fashioned vegetable garden regular rhubarb is. This handsome perennial is the original cut-and-come-again garden plant and deserves a well-loved spot in the cook's garden. Rhubarb, often paired with apples, has always provided the basis for sweet, stewed fruit desserts when they were essential family fare. Rhubarb is also the favourite resting place of snails after they have created havoc among the vegetable seedlings.

Rhubarb deserves some room among your flowers and vegetables if you're partial to its flavour. Why should future generations be denied the memory of rhubarb crumble and snail searches?

in the garden

Rhubarb needs very rich soil and full sun or at least sun for half a day. Add large quantities of manure and a nitrogen-rich fertiliser like pelleted poultry manure. Rhubarb also likes regular watering but needs a well-drained site or its roots will rot. A position somewhere near the garden hose, a leaky tap or a dripper outlet on an irrigation system is ideal.

The small leaves unfurl from tightly crinkled bundles and soon resemble elephant ears. The stems thicken, lengthen and multiply as the plant expands to cover 1m (3') or more of the garden. It can be grown in a large pot but take care to keep it well watered.

Start to harvest the outside leaves as soon as there are 5 or so replacement stems unfurling in the centre of the plant. Pull each stem down and twist sideways to break it off with a snap. Wash well to remove dirt, cut off the leaves and add them to your compost.

NEVER EAT THE LEAVES as they are poisonous.

Give regular extra feeds with liquid fertiliser and break off any flower stems that form. When rhubarb starts to fade for winter, mulch with manure and compost ready for the following spring and to protect from winter frosts. Divide the root mass every couple of years (these make terrific presents for friends and potted plants to sell at local stalls).

Rhubarb with red stems is the most familiar and most coveted variety among both gardeners and cooks. Look for plants in small pots at nurseries or plant stalls during summer or as root clusters in winter where you will have to ask the grower which colour they are. However, don't worry too much about the colour as the green-stemmed and pinkish-stemmed varieties have the same flavour and are just as good to eat.

PRESERVING THE CROP

STORING Remove the leaves and wrap the stalks in plastic in the refrigerator. Do not wash until ready to use. After a week it will go limp.

FREEZING Washed, blanched and chopped rhubarb freezes well (up to 6 months) (see Freezing, page 117). You can open-freeze or store in freezer containers. Rhubarb can also be combined with a sugar syrup with or without flavourings and frozen in containers. Stewed or pureed rhubarb freezes well (for about 9 months) and is great for almost instant desserts such as rhubarb fool.

PICKLING You can make relishes from rhubarb, combining it with other fresh and dried fruits – dates are good. Add spices, sugar (either brown or white) and vinegar to taste (see Bottling, page 118).

for the table

to prepare...

Wash rhubarb stalks and chop into short lengths. Add to a heavy-based pan with sugar and cook, over low heat, stirring constantly.

Rhubarb can be microwaved, but needs the addition of a little water.

to serve

Make a compote with stewed rhubarb, plumped dried figs and apples to serve with anything from breakfast pancakes to a plain cake.

The old favourite, rhubarb fool, is made by mixing stewed rhubarb with whipped cream and a little cardamom – the only foolish thing is to not try it.

Rhubarb bakes beautifully under a crumble topping. Orange segments and pears and your favourite spice will add extra interest.

Arrange uncooked rhubarb over a firm cake batter before baking. It will sink and create an attractive top. Brush the warm cake with melted butter and sprinkle over cinnamon or ginger sugar. Great as muffins too!

Add cooked rhubarb to home-made ice-cream. It will dye the ice-cream a pretty pink and the flavour is to die for.

rhubarb, apple and berry galette

2¹/₂ cups (375g) plain flour

2 tablespoons caster sugar

200g unsalted butter, chopped

¹/₄ cup (60g) sour cream

¹/₂ cup (125ml) milk

¹/₄ cup (40g) icing sugar

FILLING

10 medium rhubarb stems (750g), chopped

2 medium Granny Smith apples (300g), peeled, cored and chopped

250g strawberries, halved

1¹/₄ cups (275g) caster sugar

1 teaspoons vanilla essence

¹/₃ cup (50g) plain flour

PROCESS FLOUR, sugar and butter until it looks like fine sand. Add sour cream and milk and process until mixture forms a ball. Wrap in plastic and refrigerate for 30 minutes.

COVER A LARGE PIZZA TRAY (30cm or 12" across) with non-stick baking paper. Roll out the pastry to form a rough 37cm (about 15") circle. Place dough on baking tray, pile filling onto pastry leaving 5cm (2") edges. Bring pastry edges over filling and pleat to form an open pie.

SIFT THE ICING SUGAR over galette. Bake in a moderately hot oven for 1 hour and 10 minutes or until the pastry is crisp, the filling is broken down and the juices have evaporated (juices from the fruit will probably run onto the tray, but don't worry as they will become toffee by the end of the cooking time).

COOL ON THE TRAY for 20 minutes, then slide onto a wire rack. Serve warm or at room temperature with ice-cream or custard.

FILLING Combine all ingredients in a large bowl; allow to stand for about 10 minutes or until the fruit looks moist.

Serves 8–10.

Galette can be made several hours ahead. Store, covered, at room temperature.

Galette is not suitable to freeze.

sweet corn

Corn planted in blocks ensures the pollen from the tassels falls onto the silks below.

Originally used as stockfeed and for flour, sweet corn has now been bred to be a treat for humans. And what a treat it is: sweet, juicy and chewy. Those who grow sweet corn at home know how tender and sweet it can be when eaten fresh. The all-important sugar starts to convert to starch as soon as a cob is picked, hence sayings such as "walk slowly to pick it; run back to the kitchen to cook it".

It is remarkable what a difference even just a couple of hours makes to home-harvested corn. Imagine what's happening to the sweet corn that is harvested, sent to market, distributed and then arranged on a grocer's shelves. You can understand why freshly picked cobs from the garden taste so superior to anything you might buy. Give it a go; grow your own.

in the garden

Corn must grow without frost, so plant seeds indoors if your spring is not to be trusted. If you use peat or grow-pots, you can nestle the seedlings directly into the soil leaving the young roots undisturbed. Where growing conditions are milder, plant seeds directly in the garden as the soil starts to warm. In the tropics this is a year-round possibility.

Always plant corn in full sun and out of strong winds. Make sure the soil is rich in organic matter and add a complete plant food 2 weeks before planting.

Corn must be grown in blocks so the pollen from the male tassels at the top of each plant can dust the female silks on other plants as they appear on the immature cobs. The cobs form between the leaves and the stem and there can be 2, 3 or 4 to each stem. Plant seeds 40–50cm (16–20") apart in a block, clusters or circles (never in a single straight line).

Corn also requires regular deep watering for the plants to develop fully. Test with your finger that the water is soaking down deeply. This also lets you check that stilt roots are developing. These are extra support props and a means of drawing up extra water and nutrients. Hill up extra soil around these roots. The furrows created also become irrigation channels to flood the plants once or twice a week.

Spray the plants with liquid fertiliser every 2 weeks.

In 3–4 months cobs should be ready to harvest. There are 2 indicators of readiness: the silks will turn brown and the cobs will stand out from the stem. Pull down the top part of the husks and press a fingernail into the kernels. The grains should be soft and the juice creamy, not watery. When ready, pull down the cob and twist to snap it from the stem.

Where conditions remain hot, plant a second crop in early summer.

If you want baby corn cobs for Asian dishes, you can peel back the young silks and pick the immature cobs when you think they're right. However, baby corn is actually a specialised cultivar and if you want to grow this crop, you'll need to seek out special seed.

pests and diseases

Watch for aphids on the stems and hose off, crush by hand or use a spray. Ear worms can bore into the cobs from the top, chewing first at the silks. Both chemical and organic insecticide sprays (see page 9) will reduce them or crush the corn tops with your fingers at the first sign of an attack.

for the table

to prepare...

↝ Corn cobs can be boiled, steamed, barbecued or roasted. If boiling, add to a pan of boiling water for about 10 minutes (or only a few minutes if freshly picked). Don't add salt as this toughens the corn. It's not necessary to add a teaspoon of sugar, as of old, because new varieties are much sweeter.

↝ When cutting corn niblets or kernels from the cob, cut the cobs in half crossways to make them easier to handle and the niblets are less likely to end up all over the kitchen.

↝ Make stock from the denuded cobs. Simmer with traditional stock ingredients such as peppercorns and bay leaves. Use in corn-flavoured soups, casseroles and risottos.

↝ Microwave corn cobs in their husks for 3–4 minutes each or, again with husks on, barbecue them for 10 minutes, turning twice.

to serve...

↝ Discard the silk from the cobs and drizzle with a little flavoured oil, re-wrap in the husk, pile into a large baking dish, cover loosely with foil and bake in a very hot oven for about 10 minutes or until just tender.

↝ Add corn niblets to a pancake batter for corn fritters. Serve with crispy bacon, roasted tomatoes and rocket.

↝ Remove the silk from inside the cob and replace with a smear of your favourite flavoured butter. Re-wrap in its husk and barbecue until tender.

↝ Cut cob into thick slices and add to beef or chicken casseroles for the last 20 minutes of cooking.

↝ Crush niblets until slightly creamy and add to a cheese soufflé mixture.

↝ Chicken and corn seem to marry very well. The next time you stir-fry chicken, add a handful of corn kernels to the wok a few minutes before the end of the cooking time.

PRESERVING THE CROP

STORING Use as soon as possible after picking as corn loses its natural sweetness quickly. If you must store, wrap in a damp tea-towel, husk, silk and all, in the refrigerator. It will last for about 2 days, after which it will start to become dry and starchy.

FREEZING If freezing, the cobs can be left whole, cut into 7.5cm (3") lengths or cut into niblets. All need blanching before freezing (see Freezing, page 117). Freeze for up to 6 months.

PICKLING Corn relish is an old favourite, and also a good way to preserve a large crop. Cut off the niblets. Simmer with capsicums, onion, sugar, vinegar and flavourings for 30 minutes. Stir in plain flour combined with powdered mustard and turmeric (it keeps the golden colour) and a little cold water. Boil for 5 minutes. Pour into hot sterilised jars (see Bottling, page 118) and seal while hot. Store in the refrigerator for about a month.

FRESHLY PICKED AND READY TO EAT

summer fruit

Passionfruit develop from the tiny embryos in the flower centres and ripen from green to purple.

Fruit is superb in summer: richly coloured, plentiful and sweetly perfumed. With so many vegetables available all year round, summer fruits remain one of the few truly seasonal taste delights. We look forward to the shiny brightness of the first-season cherries, the wafting aroma of peaches, the dusty gleam of plums and the lush juiciness of gooseberries.

Their delights are also fleeting. Summer fruits have a short season so harvest your garden's fruits with speed and dedication. Preserve, bottle, freeze or pickle your fruits to extend their perfection into winter.

passionfruit

Passionfruit (or granadillas) enjoy life in tropical and subtropical gardens. It can be a battle to grow them without protection in cooler areas, and in frost-prone climates, a heated glasshouse is the only way. Their dark evergreen vines look handsome indeed scrambling over fences and walls, and their flowers are spectacular.

Seedlings and grafted plants are available during spring and summer. Plant in a sunny site protected from harsh winds and against a trellised wall, pergola or archway to climb over with access underneath for harvesting. Be prepared for this area to become "hallowed" ground as passionfruit don't like their surface roots to be disturbed and must be kept well watered and mulched. This is particularly true of grafted plants because, where roots are damaged, the vigorous understock will shoot up and very quickly overcome the grafted vine. Soil should be rich in organic manure or compost and given extra dressings of complete garden fertiliser each spring and late summer.

The vine grows quickly in warm weather. Direct the stems where you want them to climb and cut out any that are superfluous. The tendrils will cling to any support. Watch out for their spreading ways and prune, if necessary.

In their first winter they'll slow down and perhaps drop some leaves. Don't prune or disturb them while they're resting. The following spring the vine will get marching again and buds and flowers will develop. The flowers are green, purple and white extravagances with a tiny, immature fruit among the stamens and anthers. Bees and the breezes will do their duty and, by early summer, the first season's crop will be ready to drop off the vine.

As soon as the fruit is finished, prune the stems as it's the new growth that bears flowers. A passionfruit vine will crop well for several years and then start to fade. Then it's time to plant a replacement vine, either as a seedling raised from dropped fruit or a new grafted specimen.

pests and diseases

Aphids will mass on tender new shoots. They can be hosed or crushed if you can reach them or sprayed with an insecticide. See page 9 for alternatives to chemical sprays. Passionfruit is also attacked by a virus that produces woody-skinned fruit. It can't be treated and vines should be burnt to limit its spread. Healthy plants and grafted plants will usually be disease-resistant.

stone fruit

All stone fruits belong to the *Prunus* family. They turn on a glorious blossom display in spring, bring forth their divine fruit in high summer, offer another colour burst in autumn when their leaves turn, and then stand stark and structural through the winter.

They all demand similar growing conditions: a cool-to-cold winter, a warm summer, rich soil and a good supply of water. They are ideally suited to Mediterranean climates as long as extra water is available during dry summers. In temperate and cool temperate gardens late-spring frosts can ruin early blossoms. Some cultivars are more suited to mild subtropical zones. Ask for recommendations at your local nursery.

The spring blossoms are very delicate, so don't plant where strong winds can shatter them before the bees have had a chance to visit.

Apply a complete garden fertiliser (a proprietary blend or combined pelleted poultry manure and fish emulsion fertiliser) twice a year, in early spring and late summer. In winter when the trees are dormant, add a generous mulch of manure as well.

There are number of diseases that await stone fruit. The leaves may be twisted and deformed by leaf curl, a fungus disease that can only be treated when the tree is dormant. Pick off and burn any affected leaves during summer and autumn and give the tree extra fertiliser to promote new leaf growth in summer. Rake up the leaves regularly but don't compost them. During late winter, as early buds swell, spray with a fungicide like Bordeaux mixture. Don't spray too late as it will burn the leaves.

Aphids cause a similar wrinkling but are visible on the stem tips. Crush by hand or hose off. Fruit-fly is also a major pest. Spray a proprietary insecticide or one of our non-chemical alternatives on page 9. Boil or burn the infected fruit and collect all fallen fruit to ensure the grubs can't pupate in the soil.

cherries

Cherries are the first summer fruit on the scene.

They like cold winters and warm summers. Late frosts will ruin a whole year's crop. They also require regular watering so the fruit develops evenly. Cherries are usually self-sterile; that is, they need two or more varieties for fertilisation of the blossoms to occur. However, 'Stella' and 'Morello' can be grown on their own as they don't need another pollinator.

STORING Store a few stone fruits, enough for each day, at room temperature for the best flavour, store the remaining fruit in the refrigerator. Bring to room temperature before eating.

Pick berries just before using. If you have to pick them to beat snails and birds, store in the refrigerator in a covered container lined with absorbent paper. Avoid washing.

Passionfruit lasts for about a week at room temperature.

FREEZING All stone fruits and berries can be frozen as purees (see Freezing, page 117). Don't sweeten in case you want to make a sauce for chicken or other meats. The puree keeps, frozen, for up to a year.

Passionfruit is one of the few fruits that maintain their sharp-sweet flavour after freezing. To store, freeze the pulp in ice-cube trays, then transfer to a freezer bag. It can be frozen for up to a year.

PICKLING Stone fruits make excellent chutneys and relishes. Add dried fruit, spices, sugar and vinegar and simmer for about an hour. Spoon into hot sterilised jars and seal while hot (see Bottling, page 118).

PHOTO: DR ANDREW GRANGER

STONE FRUITS RIPENED ON THE TREE HAVE THE BEST FLAVOUR

Cherries develop into large trees and may be too large for a home garden but they do have delightful blossoms and an elegant shape. They require almost no pruning except to clear low-hanging branches.

peaches and nectarines

Peaches and their smooth-skinned cousins, nectarines, are synonymous with summer with their strong perfume and rich colouring. Different varieties are ready for picking throughout the season. There is also choice of different colours, ease of peeling and the hold of the stone.

In very cold climates peaches need a snug site near a sunny wall or even better, espaliered against it. In subtropical areas, enquire at your nursery for recommended varieties. Specially-developed dwarf forms are ideal for pots because the regular varieties won't usually crop in such confined conditions.

Peaches are self-fertile so a single tree can be planted as a garden feature, to mark a corner of the vegetable garden or shade the chicken shed. Remember not to plant where it will cast too long a shadow over vegetables in summer.

Thin the juvenile fruit and leaf shoots if heavily massed, and leave a 20cm (8") space between each for large, juicy fruit. In winter prune out crossing branches and old wood. Trim low-hanging branches and those that are too high to harvest.

Regularly clear debris from under the tree, especially after birds attack and the fruit falls. Commercial growers pick their fruit early but tree-ripened fruit is everybody's dream. Netting the tree may help deter birds.

apricots

Apricots have a delicious taste and aroma all their own. They are justifiably famous for the golden jam they produce. Apricots do best where the summers are long and hot, but are reasonably adaptable to site as there are varieties to suit coastal, highland and inland zones. They are self-fertile and, with their rounded leaves and white blossoms, they are beautiful in spring.

Prune to control their height and spread. Reduce the central sections to open out the tree to gain more sunlight and air movement around the fruit.

Fruit damaged by fruit-fly is still useful for making jam. Cut out the damaged sections from the fruit and drop the waste into boiling water. Leave to cool. This can then be safely composted. The useable sections of the fruit can be weighed and made into jam, as usual. Fruit-fly damaged plums and peaches can also be rescued in this way.

plums

Plums are the most varied of all the stone fruits. The fruit can be narrow or fat, oval or cricket-ball sized; some are green-fleshed, others purple, yellow and red. Their skins are mostly glossy but a few are powdered with a white bloom. There are varieties to suit subtropical, Mediterranean and temperate gardens and they are more tolerant of heavy clay soils than any other stone fruit. They don't grow in swamps but are happy at the water's edge.

RIPENING PLUMS DUSTED WITH BLOOM

Most plums are self-sterile and need a pollinator to form fruit. Two varieties that self-pollinate are cherry plums, mostly grown for their spring blossoms, and the variety called 'Santa Rosa' if you want just one tree. You can even buy different varieties grafted onto the one tree.

Pruning is not necessary for plum trees but remove those branches that grow across pathways or scrape the ground.

berries

Berries do best in areas with cool-to-cold winters, a gentle spring and a warm and very sunny summer. Those gardeners who can grow berries easily don't realise how much the climatically less-blessed envy them, despite the fact that many berries are barbed with thorns and it's often a backbreaking and hazardous task to harvest berries and keep the vines under control.

strawberries

Strawberries make pretty border plants and are happy among herbs and flowers. There are strawberry varieties to suit cold winter zones; some that produce high-yielding tropical crops and others for temperate zones.

Buy virus-free plants in summer and dig them into rich, free-draining soil. A straw mulch (hence the name) protects them during winter, suppresses weeds and keeps the fruit clear of the soil. Terracotta strawberry pots save space but they do need a lot of maintenance, in particular regular watering and extra fertiliser in each pocket.

The first summer is their establishment year. Cut off any runners, feed in late summer and autumn and cut off the leaves at the same time. Come spring, strawberries really get growing. Fruit may be early or mid-season ripening. Slugs, snails and birds will also rush to the harvest. Pellets and traps will deter slugs and snails, and nets will help stop the birds.

Plant out new runners during the third year in a new, well-prepared site for crops the following year. Pull out old plants. In the tropics, strawberries should be treated as annuals and replanted each year.

Alpine strawberries look frail but don't be deceived by their looks or name. They grow in most climates. The fruit is small but highly flavoured.

raspberries

Raspberry flowers develop at the top of tall, thorny canes. Different varieties fruit throughout summer, even into autumn. New canes, with some roots attached, can be planted in autumn or early spring when leafless. Buy canes from a nursery or collect from friends thinning their thickets.

Mulch well and add plenty of manure for abundant spring growth. Raspberries are invasive so be prepared for boundary trims with a sharp spade each spring. Each autumn cut out the dead canes and thin the rest to 5–6 canes to each plant.

Strawberries need to be tucked under leaves or netted to deter birds.

plum parfait with lime double berries

Parfait is a frozen French dessert based on egg yolks. It's traditionally served in tall, narrow glasses, but here we serve it in slices.

1/2 cup (110g) caster sugar

1/3 cup (80ml) water

4 egg yolks

4 medium blood plums (300g), stoned, pureed

300ml thickened cream

LIME DOUBLE BERRIES

1/3 cup (75g) caster sugar

1/2 cup (125ml) water

2 teaspoons finely shredded lime rind

1 tablespoon lime juice

200g raspberries

250g small strawberries, halved

COVER BASE and two opposite sides of 14cm x 21cm (5" x 8") loaf pan with foil. Combine sugar and water in a small pan, stir over low heat, without boiling, until sugar dissolves. Brush any sugar crystals from the side of pan with a wet pastry brush. Bring to boil; boil, uncovered, for 3 minutes.

BEAT EGG YOLKS in a medium heatproof bowl with electric mixer until combined. Gradually beat in sugar syrup, beat until pale and thick. Beat in plum puree. In another bowl, beat cream until thick; gently fold into plum mixture. Pour into prepared pan and cover the surface with plastic wrap. Freeze for several hours.

SERVE plum parfait topped with lime double berries.

LIME DOUBLE BERRIES Make a sugar syrup, as above, from sugar and water. Boil for 5 minutes. Allow syrup to cool to room temperature then stir in lime rind and juice with berries. Cover and refrigerate until just before required.

Serves 6–8.

Parfait can be frozen for up to a week. Lime double berries can be made several hours ahead.

blackberries and "friends"

Blackberries and "friends" are trailing berries and, like raspberries, are thorny horrors, although there are some thornless cultivars. "Friends" include loganberries, boysenberries, tayberries and youngberries. Blackberries have become weeds in Australia and must be poisoned and removed. There are approved cultivars that don't spread, so take care to choose the right one.

Attach the trailing canes to a trellis and cut off at ground level after fruiting. Tie up each new cane as it develops. This will keep the plant easy to harvest and stop it becoming a dense thicket.

gooseberries

Gooseberries grow on a spiky shrub and, if destined for cooking only, the globular, light-green fruit are picked in late spring. In summer they ripen to a perfumed, sweet, soft fruit that is eaten fresh.

Plant cuttings or plants in well-manured soil in late autumn or winter. As gooseberries are very spiky, it's best to keep them thinned out during winter and to remove any suckers to make harvesting less hazardous.

blueberries

Blueberries grow on a thornless shrub that colours delightfully in autumn. The berries ripen over late summer and into autumn. They need peaty, acid soil to do well. If you can offer this, plus a cool-to-cold winter, they are the berry for you. You can also grow them in pots with the right soil mix.

GLEAMING REDCURRANTS READY TO PICK

currants

Currants grow in grape-like clusters (red, black or white) on shrubs. Plant in autumn, winter or spring when plants are available from nurseries. Give them a protective mulch come winter if the weather is very cold. Blackcurrants fruit on new wood so cut all the stems back in winter to 10cm (4") above the soil. Red and white currants fruit on old stems so prune only as needed to shape and control the shrubs. Each spring give all currant varieties a rich dressing of manure and a complete plant food, kept clear of the stems. Repeat in late summer.

for the table

to serve...

➣ STONE FRUIT poached in their skins retain their bright colours and are easier to peel afterwards.

➣ There's nothing better than to pick a warm PASSIONFRUIT from the vine, lop off the top and eat!

➣ RASPBERRY jam that is baked rather than boiled is superbly flavoured.

➣ Add PEACH puree to the bottom of a glass of champagne.

➣ Poach PEACHES in a low-joule lemonade or ginger ale for a great summer treat for slimmers.

➣ For a beautiful upside-down cake, place chopped STONE FRUIT in the base of a cake pan along with brown sugar and butter, and top with a plain cake batter. Cook as normal and let stand for 5 minutes before turning out.

➣ Process overripe PEACHES with a little sugar until pureed. Freeze in ice-cube trays and transfer to a freezer bag. For a refreshing water-ice, simply puree as many cubes as you need.

➣ BERRIES and CHERRIES can make great-tasting, colourful vinegars for salads and sauces. Pour good-quality white wine vinegar over halved fruit and add cardamom pods or cinnamon sticks, if you like. Cover and stand for 2 days. Discard the fruit and spices and pour the flavoured vinegar into hot sterilised bottles (see Bottling, page 118). Store in the refrigerator for up to 1 year. The vinegar becomes sweeter as it ages.

➣ Poach any STONE FRUIT in a white wine sugar syrup with a little stem ginger; cool the fruit in the syrup and serve with a dollop of crème fraîche or mascarpone cheese.

➣ For a hot, sweet soufflé either place the chopped fruit in the base of the dish or add pureed APRICOTS to a basic sweet soufflé mixture.

➣ A summer fruit platter is the perfect finish to a barbecue. Arrange slices of fresh PEACHES, APRICOTS, PLUMS, NECTARINES and mangoes on a large platter; drizzle over PASSIONFRUIT pulp, sprinkle with chopped pistachios.

summer herbs

AROMATIC BASIL: QUEEN OF THE SUMMER

Summertime is the very season for herbs. Almost every herb is romping by summer. There will be generous supplies in the garden or in pots within easy reach of the cook's kitchen.

The two herbs featured: basil and mint, are at their most pungent and flavourful in the heat of the summer sun.

in the garden

basil

Basil is the queen of the summer herbs. It originally came from India even though it is now synonymous with Mediterranean cuisine. Varieties are also used throughout Asia and are added to noodles, curries and soups.

Its strong scent evokes high summer and its lush, green leaves scattered over salads and pasta captures the essence of warm weather. Its leaves are also an honest indicator of the turn of the seasons as they start to blacken and wither in cool winds.

Basil is an annual herb, but you might be lucky to find self-sown seedlings in your garden from last year. Otherwise, pots, punnets and seeds are readily available from nurseries throughout summer.

Plant seedlings in a sunny site in a rich garden bed or large pot after all frosts and cold winds have finished. If spaced 15-20cm (6-8") apart they will support each other as they grow.

Basil is lovely planted near a path or steps where you accidently brush the leaves at each passing. Pinch out the flower heads as they start to form and gather sprigs by nipping back the top of the stem to a pair of leaves. This will thicken the plant.

Feed with a liquid fertiliser every 2 weeks but spray late in the day to avoid leaf burn. Always wash the leaves before using. Slugs, snails, grasshoppers and caterpillars will want a share but most pests can be seen and caught before they've done too much damage.

mint

Mint grows in most climates all year round, although in very cool areas it will need protective mulch during winter. But in summer mint really romps, growing tall, flowering and extending invasive new stems underground to take control of your herb bed.

The best form of control is confinement in pots or troughs. These can be dug into the garden with their rims above the soil, but always watch out for stems that escape over the edge.

The scent of mint is delightful and there are a number of varieties – common garden mint with its mild flavour and rounded leaves, apple mint with its furry foliage, spearmint with its glossy pointed leaves, and peppermint with slightly purple-toned leaves. 'Eau-de-cologne' is named because of its perfume and, although not used in the kitchen, it's lovely to brush past.

Mint loves water and grows best with regular supplies; it will, however, recover if forgotten. Mint is much more aromatic if grown in full sun but it does tolerate partial shade. Flowers are mauve, cream or white. Give it a "haircut" after it flowers.

Vietnamese mint or laksa herb grows in the same generous way as mint but is not a mint at all. Its strong flavour is not dissimilar to coriander and can be used as a substitute. It is, of course, added to laksas. Cut away the midrib if it gets woody and replace plants each spring.

for the table

to serve...

⟿ BASIL is a must with tomatoes. Leaves are best torn, not cut. Scatter over tomatoes and drizzle with olive oil.

⟿ Add BASIL to any dish. To fully enhance its flavour, stir in extra fresh leaves at the end of cooking.

⟿ BASIL pesto is justifiably famous. Stir into soups and stews at the last minute, or spread on crusty bread before toasting for bruschetta. A pizza base spread with pesto under the tomato base is delicious.

⟿ Place whole BASIL leaves over the centre of a boned loin of pork, cover with seasoning, roll and roast. Also add basil to the gravy for extra flavour.

⟿ A great dressing for a lamb salad is pureed BASIL with a green apple, garlic, lemon juice and oil.

⟿ MINT cooked with apples makes a traditional mint jelly. Cook apples until they go rosy pink but don't strain the pulp through muslin or the result will be cloudy.

⟿ MINT mixed with low-fat yogurt, garlic and seeded cucumbers serves as a dip or as a sauce over grilled fish or chicken.

⟿ Wrap whole MINT leaves, prawns and julienne vegetables in Thai rice paper rounds and serve with a lemon grass and mint sauce.

⟿ Freeze MINT leaves in ice-cubes and add to long cool drinks.

⟿ Serve zucchini and MINT fritters with Really Useful Sauce (see page 39).

PRESERVING THE CROP

STORING Pick herbs as close to using as possible. Basil, in particular, is very fragile and blackens easily. Store in a plastic bag wrapped loosely in absorbent paper towel for up to 3 days.

FREEZING Both mint and basil can be frozen (see Freezing, page 117) for up to 6 months. Freeze sprigs in a rigid container and pluck off the frozen leaves as you need them. Once frozen, basil and mint are best used in cooked dishes.

Another good idea is to chop basil finely, mix with butter and freeze as a log. Slice off a portion as you need it.

DRYING Dried basil has not much flavour and has limited uses in the kitchen. Dried mint (see Drying, page 119) is used widely in teas, often mixed with chamomile.

COOLING MINT AND LIME DRINK

Autumn

AUTUMN PROVIDES A RICH HARVEST

Autumn
garden diary

The delights of summer inevitably fade.

Days begin to shorten and the first signs of autumn start to appear. Mornings and evenings are that bit cooler, and a warm spot in the sun is soon a sought-out pleasure. There's no denying the altered slant of the sun and the changes in the garden as plants prepare for the approach of winter, more spectacular in some parts of the world than others, but observable everywhere, from the subtropics to the polar reaches. In the tropics there'll be lush new growth in response to the abundant rain, but elsewhere there's a sedate reduction, a battening down for the lean times ahead.

But with autumn come the best conditions for working in the garden, clearing up the debris, the straggling leftovers and the dried remains that can all be composted when not diseased. If you have mountains of fallen leaves, pile them in a corner with handfuls of nitrogen-rich fertiliser, weigh them down with netting or a tarpaulin and leave them to mature for summer mulch.

Deep digging and spreading around manure or compost to revitalise gardens becomes a pleasure in the cool weather. If you've got areas that are becoming shaded as the sun dips, leave them deeply mulched with manure and straw or grass clippings until the spring.

Plant out ready-prepared or bought seedlings to guarantee winter supplies. It is often a good idea to keep a record of what grew where in the garden over summer, what was successful, what caused more trouble than it was worth and what was not a treat to eat.

Prune back shrubs and trees that block sunlight or lean over too far. Perennial vegetables like artichokes, chillies, capsicums and asparagus will benefit from pruning before being mulched for protection against frost.

Check that the soil is well drained as winter chill in soggy soil can cause root rot and stunted growth. Build up soil levels with mulch and compost or put in drains where water will lie for any length of time.

And enjoy your time in the kitchen drying, preserving and storing your summer bounty.

pick now...

MOST GARDENS

- apples
- artichokes
- broccoli
- cabbage
- carrots
- chillies
- early citrus
- grapes
- Jerusalem artichokes
- kiwi fruit
- leeks
- lettuce
- melons
- olives
- pears
- pumpkins
- silverbeet
- spinach
- and all summer crops still producing

plant now...

MOST GARDENS

- Asian greens
- beetroot
- broad beans
- broccoli
- Brussels sprouts
- cabbage
- cauliflower
- endive
- lettuce
- mizuna
- onion
- peas
- radicchio
- radish
- rocket
- silverbeet
- spinach

CLOCKWISE FROM TOP LEFT Autumn weather makes gardening jobs a pleasure; fully ripe melons have the best colour and flavour; muddy boots kicked off before tramping dirt indoors; gloriously coloured Turkish Turbans are both ornamental and very useful pumpkins; pears are picked when they break off easily from the tree while still firm and are ripe to eat when they yield to pressure at the stem end.

globe artichokes

FLOWER BUDS READY TO HARVEST

Who would believe that a thistle could look and taste so good? Globe artichokes belong to the thistle family, and are the flower buds of a wonderful grey-leafed plant that contributes a stunning architectural element to any flower-bed or vegetable patch. Subtle they are not; artichoke plants are tall and dramatic and require almost 1m (3') of space all round for their branches to spread. Try them if you have space.

in the garden

Provide artichokes with deep, well-manured soil and plant in spring in temperate climates or late autumn or winter in milder gardens. Well-rooted offshoots from an established plant may be available from friends or as plants from large nurseries. Artichokes are perennials, so once planted, they'll last 3–4 years. Treat them as annuals in frosty gardens by raising fresh seed indoors or under glass, and planting them out as soon as the frosts are over.

Give artichokes side dressings of complete garden fertiliser or pelleted poultry manure to ensure strong growth and buds at each branch end.

Cut the buds when they are still tightly closed and about 5–6cm (2–2¹/₂") round. Don't leave the globes on the plant too long as a dry thistle top will develop and other buds will not form once flowering begins. If you reduce the number of buds on the stems as soon as they start to develop, you'll force fewer, but larger, globes.

After flowering, keep artichokes watered and in autumn cut the stems back to 30cm (12") above the soil. Spread around a protective and nourishing mulch of lucerne hay and manure for the winter and to give them a good start come spring.

for the table

to prepare...

~ When preparing artichokes there's no need to snip off the top third of the leaves unless you are bothered by their tattiness or they are the variety with a small spike at the end of each leaf. Always remove the tough bottom leaves. Rub any cut surface with a lemon as artichokes discolour rapidly.

PRESERVING THE CROP

STORING Although artichokes are best eaten soon after harvest, they can be stored, unwashed in a vegetable storage bag in the refrigerator for up to 4 days. Wash just before using.

FREEZING The hearts can be blanched and frozen (see Freezing, page 117). Break away the outside leaves and blanch hearts in acidulated water; drain well. Freeze for up to 4 months.

PICKLING Artichoke hearts can be cooked in spiced vinegar and stored in olive oil (see Bottling, page 118) for about 3 months. Toss the cooked hearts in herbs before covering with olive oil.

artichokes with lemon pepper hollandaise

1¹/₂ cups (375ml) water

1 cup (250ml) white wine

¹/₃ cup (80ml) olive oil

4 bay leaves

6 medium globe artichokes (1.2kg), trimmed

LEMON PEPPER HOLLANDAISE

3 egg yolks

2 teaspoons grated lemon rind

1¹/₂ tablespoons lemon juice

¹/₂ teaspoon cracked black pepper

250g unsalted butter

COMBINE water, wine, oil and bay leaves in a non-reactive pan, bring to the boil. Add artichokes, simmer, covered 30 minutes or until tender. Drain, discard liquid. Split artichokes lengthways and scoop out the hairy choke. Serve warm or at room temperature with lemon pepper hollandaise.

LEMON PEPPER HOLLANDAISE Blend egg yolks, rind, juice and pepper until combined. Melt butter in a small pan, heat until bubbling. Slowly add hot butter to egg yolk mixture, with motor operating, until mixture is thick and creamy. Avoid adding the milk residue from the butter.

Serves 6.

Artichokes can be prepared an hour ahead. Lemon pepper hollandaise is best made close to serving.

⮑ You may like to remove the choke. Pull the centre leaves apart and, using a teaspoon, dig out the hairy choke and some of the tiny inner leaves.

⮑ Boil, steam or microwave until just tender. Always cook artichokes in a non-reactive pan, or your artichokes will blacken.

to serve...

⮑ Most artichoke recipes call for dipping the leaves in sauces. The Italian sauce, bagna cauda, with anchovies is great but hollandaise goes just as well.

⮑ Artichokes can be stuffed and baked. Try a mixture of breadcrumbs, pancetta and basil or oregano. Place stuffing between the artichoke leaves and bake. Drizzle with a flavoured mayonnaise and, again, add a few anchovies for their salty taste.

⮑ Add cooked and quartered artichokes to salads, especially Mediterranean ones. Add a touch of mint to the vinaigrette for a refreshing flavour.

⮑ Top chicken fillets with cooked artichoke hearts, pour over cheese sauce, sprinkle with parmesan and mozzarella and grill until golden and bubbling.

⮑ Serve artichokes hearts on toasted foccacia. Drizzle with garlic oil.

⮑ Do not discard the stem of young artichokes. About 15cm (6") is edible. Cook with the heads, then peel and slice, and add to dishes in the final stages.

avocado

PICKED FIRM, AVOCADOS RIPEN INDOORS

PHOTO: © NSW AGRICULTURE

Avocados were once exotic tropical fruits that few people knew how to peel, let alone grow and present at the table. Then there was a rush of extravagant uses from ice-cream to heated dishes. Now we've settled for the "simple is best" belief to take advantage of the rich, buttery smoothness of avocados and their delightful green colouring.

in the garden

This elegant, evergreen tree grows to about 8m (25') and may be too large for the average garden. It also demands a warm and frost-free site. If in a well-sheltered position, an avocado tree can be coddled along in cooler conditions.

Avocados display the most peculiar behaviour: in spring the flowers change sex on the same trees and it is often necessary to grow compatible varieties to achieve effective pollination. If you plan to grow a few, combine 'Sharwill', a mid-season fruiter with 'Hass', a late variety and you will ensure effective pollination and an extended harvesting period. Seek advice from your local nursery. Plant trees in spring to give them summer to get established. Like mangoes, avocado seeds might sometimes, very occasionally, sprout from compost heaps but such trees can be unreliable and very slow to fruit.

Apply a good dressing of complete garden fertiliser or pelleted poultry manure under the drip line in spring, summer and autumn every year, and water in well. Avocados don't need pruning unless you're trying to keep the branches at a reasonable picking height.

Avocados bloom in late winter and spring, and the fruit forms over summer.

The fruit doesn't ripen on the tree. They are ready to pick when they've ceased expanding and have started to lose their glossy sheen. They don't need a sunny spot to ripen. They are fully ripe when they just give to pressure at the stem end. Otherwise, you can leave the fruit on the tree until they fall to the ground, collect them and bring them inside to ripen. Pests such as possums can be destructive, chewing the bark and eating the unripe fruit.

for the table

to prepare...

∿ You can speed up the ripening process by putting an avocado in a brown paper bag with a ripe banana. The ethylene gas given off by the banana helps ripen the avocado.

Avocados discolour quickly once cut so the addition of acid is necessary. Lemon or lime juice or vinegar will do the job. Slice or chop the avocado as required in the recipe and toss in a little juice or vinegar to keep its colour.

to serve...

Add slices of avocado, coated in lemon juice, to green salads where they will add a buttery texture and taste.

Mash avocado with lemon juice, add chopped tomato and some shredded coriander leaves for a great topping for nachos or tacos.

The space left by the avocado stone is perfect for filling. Although it's now considered passé to serve avocado seafood, the opportunity seems too good to pass up. Fresh flaked crab mixed with lime juice, a little chilli and some garlic hits the spot.

Use mashed avocado as a spread on salad sandwiches in place of butter or margarine.

Small, date-sized avocadoes are unfertilised fruits and are sold as cocktail avocados. They are great served with creamy fillings as finger food. But be warned: they are fiddly to peel and do discolour so need to be coated with lemon or lime juice first.

Make creamy salad dressings by pureeing avocado with herbed vinaigrette, drizzle over salads or add dollops to a cooked pizza. Yum!

PRESERVING THE CROP

STORING Avocados are difficult to store at their peak of ripeness. They can be stored at room temperature for several days. If you have a glut of ripe avocados, store them in the refrigerator for a few days and the cold will slow the ripening process.

FREEZING Avocados do not freeze and cannot be bottled, so must be enjoyed fresh.

PHOTO: LEIGH CLAPP

The simplest lunches are often the most perfect.

pumpkin

STRONG-FLAVOURED 'GOLDEN NUGGETS'

These ragged but ornamental wanderers have developed throughout summer and by autumn or even early winter will be ready to harvest. Some pumpkins are coloured a subtle grey like the Queensland Blue or Jarrahdale; others are deep green and flecked like the Jap or Turkish Turban, and others are orange to cream like the Butternut, Jack Little or Red Kuri. These all have rich orange flesh and are excellent to eat.

Huge, competition-size pumpkins are spectacular but are mostly used for stockfeed. The shapes and sizes of pumpkins are as varied as their colours.

in the garden

Pumpkins belong to the same family as the large and diverse range of melons, cucumbers, zucchini and squash and require the same growing and cultivation conditions (see pages 42–43 and 54–55).

If you have the space, let your pumpkins run wild over fences, sheds or trees. This will save ground space in the garden. Make sure the fruits don't get rubbed by trees or against fences as the skin gets damaged and scarred. The developing fruits may need support as well, if growing on a fence or high place.

Some suggestions are given on page 42 for controlling the spread of cucurbits generally. Some compact forms are available, usually marketed as "bush" pumpkins that cluster around a central stem. These are ideal for growing in limited spaces or pots. Pumpkins must have regular water during their development, particularly when confined in pots.

Pumpkins are the only member of the large cucurbit group to be harvested after the vine has withered and after the attachment point has broken or at least become woody and brittle. Dry and harden them in the sun if they have to be harvested earlier. They must be fully mature for good flavour and the skin hardened to ensure they will keep.

Always check stored pumpkins regularly for signs of rot or pest damage. See pages 43 and 55 for the control of pests and diseases.

for the table

to prepare...

⌒ Make pumpkin slightly easier to peel and still retain all your fingers by microwaving for a few seconds after cutting into pieces. Otherwise, call in some muscle.

PRESERVING THE CROP

STORING Uncut pumpkins keep for months. Store in a cool, dry place. Inspect often to see if any blemished or soft patches have developed. If so, cut these away and use the pumpkin at once. When cut, remove the seeds and inside fibres and store in the refrigerator.

FREEZING Uncooked pumpkin is not suitable to freeze. But pumpkin puree and pumpkin soup freeze beautifully (see Freezing, page 117).

PICKLING With the addition of sugar, citrus rind and juice and flavourings, such as fresh herbs, pumpkin can be made into jam. Seal in hot, sterilised jars for up to 4 months (see Bottling, page 118).

Make chutney from pumpkin, apples and raisins with spices, vinegar and sugar. Keeps for up to 6 months.

to serve...

~ Add chunks of roasted pumpkin to pasta sauces or, if you're keen, make your own ravioli from roasted pumpkin, sage and parmesan cheese.

~ There's no need to add cream to pumpkin soup. Simply cook chunks in chicken or vegetable stock with added aromatics such as onion and garlic. Puree and serve with bacon and pan-fried bread. A little added orange rind and juice will bring out the natural sweetness of the pumpkin.

~ Make a gratin from thinly sliced pumpkin, kumara and potato. Pour over a little cream, sprinkle with herbs, breadcrumbs and cheese, and bake.

~ Pumpkin makes great deep-fried chips, but watch carefully as they cook faster than potatoes.

~ Like zucchini flowers, pumpkin flowers are edible. Remove the inside stamens and fill with a cheese mixture. Dip in a light batter and deep-fry until golden. Otherwise, use whole and add to frittatas.

~ The seeds of pumpkin are also edible. Dry them and discard the shell. The kernels are known as pepitas and have a nutty flavour that goes well with browned butter. Serve over grilled fish.

~ Cut the tops off mini pumpkins, add a dot of butter and drizzle with honey; replace the top and bake until tender.

roasted pumpkin and rosemary risotto

When you cook a roast, cook extra pumpkin to add to salads or dishes like this.

1kg pumpkin, chopped

1/4 cup (60ml) olive oil

1 1/2 cups (300g) arborio rice

1 clove garlic, crushed

1 tablespoon rosemary leaves

4 cups (1 litre) chicken or vegetable stock, hot

150g baby spinach leaves

1/4 cup (20g) coarsely grated parmesan cheese

1/4 cup (60ml) cream

COMBINE PUMPKIN and half the oil in a baking dish and cook in a moderate oven for about 40 minutes or until pumpkin is tender.

HEAT REMAINING OIL in a large pan; add rice, stir for 2 minutes or until the rice is coated in oil. Add garlic and rosemary and cook stirring until fragrant. Add the stock, in batches, stirring constantly over low heat until each addition of stock is absorbed before adding the next. Stir in cooked pumpkin, spinach, cheese and cream. Stir over heat until hot.

Serves 4.

Make risotto close to serving. Leftover risotto can be made into patties and pan-fried. Serve topped with crisp prosciutto and dot with sour cream.

carrots

PRESERVING THE CROP

STORING Store carrots in vegetable storage bags in the refrigerator. Baby carrots will keep for 2–3 days while larger carrots can be kept for about a week.

FREEZING Carrots can be blanched and frozen whole, if baby, or otherwise sliced (see Freezing, page 117) for up to 10 months. Grated carrot can also be blanched and frozen but doesn't keep as long. It's useful to have on hand to add to casseroles and stir-fries.

PICKLING Carrots can also be pickled. Cook for a very short time only and pack into hot sterilised jars (see Bottling, page 118), pour over a hot, spiced vinegar mixture and seal while hot. Leave for a couple of weeks before serving with antipasto platters or ploughman's lunches. They will keep for up to 6 months.

GREEN-TOPPED CARROTS ARE JUST AS EDIBLE AS THE ORANGE-TOPPED

Why bother growing carrots? They're cheap and plentiful in the supermarket, after all. Yet these colourful and familiar vegetables are ideal for growing in backyard gardens. Their soft, feathery green tops look great among the other crops and they don't take up much space. There are even short, round varieties that grow happily in pots.

Carrots have many uses. They are the indispensable vegetable for casseroles, stews, soups and stocks; they are delicious on their own, with chopped parsley, eaten raw, grated in salads, julienned in stir-fries, baked into cakes and are universally admired as a juice vegetable par excellence. You'll never wonder what to do with your bumper crop of carrots.

in the garden

The delicate foliage of carrots is a clue to their fragile constitution. They are frost-tender, so don't plant in autumn where the winters are cold. Nor do they like hot, dry weather. Autumn and early spring are ideal times for sowing in Mediterranean, subtropical and frost-free temperate gardens.

Like all root crops, carrots like a soft soil mix. Break up all clods and reduce all organic matter to fine particles otherwise they'll be misshapen where the going's too tough. Add a general garden fertiliser or pelleted poultry manure as the soil is worked over. Drag through a trowel or press on a rake handle to form shallow furrows for the seeds. Carrot seeds are very fine and tend to stick together. They can be mixed with fine sand to distribute them evenly. Otherwise, lightly roughen up the soil in the furrow after the seeds have been dropped in. Seedlings emerge in 2–3 weeks. Sometimes carrots are sown with radish seeds, which are much larger. The radishes germinate sooner, their leaves keep weeds at bay while the carrots are immature, and they are harvested well before they begin to compete with the carrots for root space.

Thin when the seedlings are tiny and again as small carrots start to form. These are the tiny foretastes of the gatherings to come. Leave 5cm (2") between the remaining carrots to allow enough room for their ultimate size. Keep well watered, weed-free and hill up the soil if the carrot tops start to show above the soil. Sunlight turns carrots green. They are still edible, but look less attractive.

Check their size after about 3 months. Pull out a carrot or run your fingers around the top under the soil. If it's the right size, take as many as you need for each occasion, leaving the others in the ground. However, don't leave the stragglers too long as they'll become woody. Sow follow-up plantings each month. Parsnips grow similarly.

PHOTO: AWW HOME LIBRARY

indian dhal and carrot soup

1 tablespoon peanut oil

1 medium brown onion (150g), chopped coarsely

2 cloves garlic, crushed

1 tablespoon ground cumin

1 tablespoon ground coriander

2 teaspoons garam masala

5 medium carrots (600g), chopped coarsely

8 cups (2 litres) vegetable stock

6 cups (1.5 litres) water

1/2 cup (100g) brown lentils

1/2 cup (100g) yellow split peas

1/2 cup (100g) red lentils

2 tablespoons coarsely chopped fresh coriander leaves

HEAT OIL in large saucepan; cook onion and garlic, stirring, until onion softens. Stir in cumin, coriander and garam masala, stirring, until fragrant. Add carrot; cook, stirring, 2 minutes.

STIR IN STOCK and the water; bring to the boil. Add brown lentils and peas; simmer, uncovered, 30 minutes.

ADD RED LENTILS; simmer, uncovered, about 10 minutes or until both lentils and peas are tender. Just before serving soup, stir in coriander.

Serves 6.

This soup can be made up to 3 days ahead. Store, covered, in the refrigerator or freeze for up to 2 weeks.

for the table

to prepare...

∼ There is no need to peel carrots; they'll lose most of their vitamins if you do. Just wash thoroughly and remove the tops.

∼ Carrots can be boiled, steamed or microwaved, but remember not to overdo it. They should be crisp rather than limp.

∼ Children often prefer carrots raw, and when they're just pulled from the garden and washed, they have even more appeal.

to serve...

∼ Grated carrots and fresh mint make an interesting and easy salad.

∼ Grated carrot can be added to potato cakes; serve with a dot of butter.

∼ Add grated carrot, squeezed out in kitchen paper, to a spicy apple cake. Eat while still warm.

∼ Start the day with freshly squeezed apple and carrot juice. Add pineapple juice for extra zing. Another popular combination is carrot, orange and beetroot.

olives

OLIVES RIPENING TO BLACK

PHOTO: JACQUELINE RICHARDS

Their home is land bounded by or close to the Mediterranean Sea. Most of the picturesque, gnarled specimens are hundreds of years old and still productive. Massive new groves are constantly being planted to cope with the expanding world demand for olive oil.

It's impossible to imagine Spanish, Italian, Greek and Middle Eastern cuisines without olives and olive oil. Equally impossible to imagine is the Mediterranean without its characteristic groves of olive trees with their narrow, grey-green leaves and tough, gnarled bark.

Olives vary in size and colour, but there are scores of cultivars that will provide you with just the type to suit your garden. Olives are not palatable straight from the tree. They have to be brined before use. They can then be bottled in brine or oil, pitted, filled or simply eaten salted.

in the garden

An olive tree's chief requirement is well-drained soil with enough depth of soil for its roots to hold, even though an olive tree is predominantly a surface rooter.

Keep olive trees well mulched (straw, decaying grass clippings, leaf mulch, even rocks) during hot, dry summers to keep moisture around the roots. For a productive life, olive trees need protection from winter winds. They grow to 4–5m quickly.

Most olives can survive frosts, occasional snowfalls and hot dry summers. There are varieties that do well in subtropical and temperate areas. Olive trees can also be grown in large pots for a dramatic display, though they will produce only a modest crop.

Discrete, fragrant olive clusters appear in early summer after their first 3–4 years' growth. The berries fill out over summer. They can be harvested green by running your hands down the fruit-laden stems. They are easier to pick when ripe and black because they naturally fall off.

In olive groves sheets are spread under the trees and the branches are shaken with a mechanical gripper which harvests the entire crop at once. For the home gardener, vigorously shaking the branches is sufficient to release the ripe olives. Pick up the olives from your dropsheet. You can also simply pick up the olives as they fall and store the early arrivals in the refrigerator until you've got sufficient numbers for brining.

Ask at your nursery for recommended cultivars for your area. One or a few olive trees make an interesting project for the keen gardener, and you can continue the ancient tradition of preserving olives at home. You will, alas, need a whole grove to keep your kitchen in olive oil for the year.

for the table

to serve...

⌁ Blend or process preserved pitted olives with anchovies, sun-dried tomatoes, capers and garlic for a spread that has to be tried to be believed. Spread alone on bruschetta (thickly cut toast) or top with goat cheese.

⌁ Once olives have been brined, pack them into hot sterilised jars with lemon grass, chillies and coriander seeds for a fragrant Asian flavour.

⌁ Wrap pitted preserved olives in a cheese pastry and chill for several hours. Bake them in a hot oven until golden and serve at room temperature with drinks.

⌁ Puree preserved, pitted olives with parmesan cheese, garlic and oregano. Spread this paste over the base of a pizza, together with cheese and sun-dried tomatoes.

⌁ Toss a few preserved olives over a watermelon and red onion salad; drizzle with orange juice and olive oil.

pickled olives

Olives need to be pickled for about 5 weeks before using. Don't mix black and green olives.

1.5kg black or green olives
1/3 cup (75g) fine sea salt
4 cups (1 litre) water
1/2 cup (125ml) olive oil

DISCARD any badly blemished olives. Using a sharp small knife, make two small slits along the length of each olive, through to the stone (some people use a hammer to lightly crack each olive). Add olives to 2-litre (8-cup) sterilised jars (see Bottling, page 118) until two-thirds full. Cover with water. Fill a small plastic bag with water; tie securely and sit on top of the olives to keep them submerged (scum will appear on the surface of the water).

CHANGE the water every day. Do this for 4 days for black olives and 6 days for green olives.

COMBINE the salt and water in a medium pan, stir over heat until salt is dissolved; let brine cool to room temperature.

DRAIN the water from jars and cover olives with brine. Pour oil over olives and brine. Seal the jars.

DO NOT disturb for 5 weeks. Keep in a cool, dry place for up to 6 months.

Making slits in olives.

Pouring water over olives in sterilised jars. The small, water-filled plastic bag keeps the olives submerged.

Pouring oil over the olives to seal.

PRESERVING THE CROP

SALTED OLIVES All olives need to be preserved in brine before consumption (when bottling do not mix black and green olives). Olives can also be salted before use as this is a form of brining. Toss the olives in an equal weight amount of salt and place in a sieve or drainer. Weigh down and leave for a month at least. The olives will be dried and have a wrinkly skin and a salty taste (you can rinse before using).

STORING Untreated olives should be kept for as little time as possible. Store in a vegetable storage bag in the refrigerator for about 2 days.

PICKLING Olives can be pickled (brined) (see recipe, previous page) and then marinated (see recipe, this page).

FREEZING Untreated or treated olives are not suitable to freeze.

marinated olives

This is the next step after the pickling (brining) process and cannot be completed unless you have brined the olives first (see recipe, previous page).

The flavourings of marinated olives can be changed to suit your taste.
Try Cajun olives: add chilli, garlic, black peppercorns, mustard seeds and celery seeds. You can also try packing sun-dried tomatoes with the olives and adding sprigs of dried oregano and some garlic.

600g drained black or green olives

1 clove garlic, sliced

2 lemon wedges

2 sprigs fresh thyme or rosemary

2 cups (500ml) olive oil

COMBINE olives, garlic, lemon and herbs in a 1-litre (4-cup) sterilised jar (see Bottling, page 118). Pour in olive oil to cover olives; seal well.

LEAVE for 2 weeks before using. Store in a cool, dark place for up to 6 months and, once opened, refrigerate for up to a month.

autumn fruit

Summer fruits are scented, sensual but oh-so-fragile. Autumn fruits are robust, dependable, earthily fragrant and often magnificently storable. Harvesting new-season fruit is always a delight but the first bite of a nature-chilled crisp apple, licking the juice of a perfectly ripe pear, smelling the heady aroma of a sun-warmed rockmelon and tracing the convoluted intrigues of a sliced fig make the season sing.

Twining vines of grapes and kiwi fruit will drape themselves with golden hues before their leaves drop. They are both such ornamental fruits that they are able to dress the table purely in their own right. And when prepared for eating, they are even better.

AUTUMNAL FRUIT PLATTER

figs

in the garden

The gnarled framework of a fig tree stands starkly bare in winter in all but very mild climates. It will happily grow in a wide range of conditions, though it may need protection where it is very cold.

Select a variety recommended for your area, either green (called white), brown or purple fruited, whatever pleases you most. The darkest fruits make the darkest jam. Little pruning is required, and fertiliser applied in spring and late summer will keep it happy.

Birds will no doubt invade during the fruiting season so nets over the tree may well be necessary – try to keep the fruit well inside the netting. Fruit ripened on the tree is the sweetest.

for the table

to serve...

~ Eat fresh.

~ Drizzle split fresh figs with maple syrup and cook under a hot grill until warmed through. Serve filled with mascarpone cheese.

~ Place figs in individual, blind-baked pastry shells; surround figs with a ground almond, sugar and egg mixture; bake for 20 minutes until the figs are soft and the mixture is set.

PRESERVING THE CROP

figs

STORING Store figs in a single layer in the refrigerator for 2 days. After this, they start to give off a sticky juice.

FREEZING Figs are not suitable to freeze.

PICKLING The season doesn't last, so preserve their flavour by making jam.

DRYING Halved figs can be oven-dried (see Drying, page 119). Set the temperature at the lowest setting and leave overnight or until dried. Store in an airtight container in a cool, dry place.

Grapes dipped in toffee make an
after-dinner treat.

PRESERVING THE CROP

grapes

STORING Store table grapes in a vegetable
storage bag in the refrigerator for a week
or so, bringing them to room temperature
before eating.

FREEZING Grapes can be frozen but must
be eaten that way and not defrosted.

PICKLING Pack grapes into hot sterilised
jars (see Bottling, page 118), pour over a
hot sugar syrup flavoured with spices and
a high proportion of liqueur, seal while hot
and store for a couple of weeks before
using. They will keep for about 6 months
at room temperature, but once opened
must be refrigerated and used quickly.
Serve with plain cakes or ice-creams.

Grapes can also be made into jelly but
need the addition of apples or a setting
agent. Pour hot jelly into hot sterilised jars
(see Bottling, page 118) and seal while hot.
Store in a cool dry place for up to a year.
Once opened, store in the refrigerator.

grapes
in the garden

Grapes grow in most climates, except the tropics. They prefer dry air rather
than humidity where they often develop mildew-spotted leaves. This problem,
however, usually arises after fruiting, so many people have successfully
grown grapes even in humid zones with varieties that can cope better in
these conditions.

There are many grape varieties: purple or white, seedless or seeded, for eating
or for wine. Your local nursery can advise on what grows well in your area.

Grapes grow very easily from cuttings. Plant them in winter and mark the site
as it's so easy to mow over the mere sticks or break them as you pass. They
will grow very easily from cuttings taken from winter prunings.

In early spring the buds become furred and fat. Once they burst into leaf, the
new stems grow at a rapid rate. The tiny bunch-of-grape flowers are sweetly
scented. Grapevine moth (or possums) may well come to dine on new foliage.
Collect moths by hand or use Dipel to remove, but the vine will usually
survive the attack. The new leaves can be used for dolmades, but remember
to wash off any sprays. In very dry weather, soak the roots once a week.

The vine is a very generous climber and can create a sheltered dining area
under a pergola in a single season, and will form a dense cover in 2 seasons.

Birds and bees will want their share so pick the grape bunches regularly and
keep the area beneath the vine clear of debris. Handle the bunches gently so
you don't remove any bloom and always cut, rather than break, the stems.

Pruning is essential in late autumn or winter if the vine is to remain
productive and shapely. For the home garden, growing it along a strong fence
or as a standard will keep it low. Cut back hard to a leaf node on sturdy wood
and remove all the cross-connecting stems. When training a grape vine to
grow high, such as over a pergola, remove all side shoots until it has reached
the desired height and a thick trunk will develop. Treat the spreading top
growth as described above.

In cold areas grapes have to be kept in a conservatory. The vines are pruned
and laid on the ground for filling with sap and speedy growth in spring.

for the table
to serve...

~ Grapes should be simply washed and enjoyed fresh. They can also be
added to tossed green salads and, of course, fruit salad.

~ Thread onto toothpicks, freeze and serve after a hot and spicy curry.

apples, pears and quinces

in the garden

These fruit, despite their differences, belong to the same family as the rose, cotoneaster and hawthorn berries, crab apples and loquats. They all retain a tiny flower remnant at the base of the fruit and prefer summers that aren't too hot and humid, and cool-to-cold winters. Some varieties tolerate other climates and these are useful to the home gardener, but major fruit production only takes place in ideal conditions.

Remember to consider summer shade and winter sun when siting fruit trees. They can be useful in your garden design, perhaps as a spreading feature, a solitary sentinel at the end of a path or as an espaliered screen.

apples

Apples like rich, deep soil and protection from strong winds that can shatter spring blossoms or damage young fruit. They don't like undrained soil; however, they do need regular watering for the fruit to fill out.

Apples are self-sterile so you'll need two trees for pollination to take place. An answer for small gardens is a grafted tree where two or three apple varieties have been inserted into the one rootstock. These can be very useful for the home gardener, if a little weird-looking, because the varieties are usually early, middle and late maturing and will produce a continuing supply rather than a once-off glut. The other alternative for tiny gardens is to espalier against a wall or grow dwarf varieties which are excellent in pots.

Keep your fingers crossed for no late-spring frosts or do what orchardists do, and turn on the sprinklers. Chase off birds that attack new buds. When the fruit starts to form, the clusters will probably include too many fruit. Some will drop off naturally but you may still have to reduce their numbers to create 10–15cm (4–5") spaces between each to provide enough room for good-sized fruit to develop. Leaving them all on will result in misshapen and skimpy apples, like the ones you find growing along roadways.

Pick apples when the flavour's right and they are crisp and juicy.

Apples store well, so pick before they develop creeping skin and birds find them. Keep the ground under the tree clear to prevent disease. Don't leave fruit lying around and rake up diseased leaves. This will reduce the incidence of codling moth in next year's fruit and fungal problems on the leaves.

Apply your preferred complete fertiliser under the tree trunk to the drip-line, and water in well each autumn and spring.

Pruning is done during winter and is essential for espaliered apples to control and shape them. Pruning can also be useful on a full-sized tree to reduce the mass of branches and open it out, vase-like, to capture extra sun and allow air to circulate around the blossoms, leaves and fruit.

THE RICH HUES OF ROSE FAMILY FRUITS

PRESERVING THE CROP

apples

STORING Store apples in the refrigerator in a vegetable storage bag to help retain crispness, although apples are best eaten at room temperature for full flavour. As a general rule, large apples do not store as well as smaller ones.

FREEZING Blanched apple wedges can be frozen for up to 3 months (see Freezing, page 117) and are useful for adding to cooked desserts such as cobblers and pies. Do not thaw before using.

PICKLING Apples make wonderful pink-coloured jellies. Place in hot sterilised jars (see Bottling, page 118) and seal while hot. Store in a cool, dark place for up to a year. Add quinces to apple jelly as well. Apples are often added to chutneys and relishes as an extender to other fruits and vegetables and a setting agent for jams and jellies.

DRYING Apples can be dried in slices but need to be prepared in a salt or citric acid solution before drying (see Drying, page 119).

A JUICY MUNCH

pears

Like apples, pears like rich soil and protection from winds. Also like apples, pears like well-drained circumstances but plenty of water, especially when the fruit is developing. During long, dry summer spells, you'll need to water to supplement nature.

Pear trees can be grown individually as they don't need a pollinator. They are usually taller and form a more pyramidal shape than apples. There's no need to prune them unless you want to reduce their height. They blossom earlier than apples and hence are more vulnerable to frost damage. So, if you have the choice of site, plant pears in your least frost-prone area. Their spring blossoms and autumn leaves are magnificent.

Pears are ready to harvest when they willingly break from the tree but are still hard. They ripen after picking, and this is their greatest disguise. Just giving in to pressure at the stem end is the most reliable clue to the readiness of pears as their outside appearance tells you very little. Perfect poker players, it's been said. They turn from perfect to wasted in no time at all, but stewing or pickling can save a few.

quinces

The large blossoms of quince in spring are handsomely restrained and the whole tree is attractive throughout the year. The fruit has a furry, golden skin, hard, white flesh and an exquisite aroma. Most flesh turns a beautiful rich pink, as if by magic, as it cooks, and all produce a claret-red liquid as they reduce to a jelly. 'Appleshape' doesn't cook to pink but 'de Bourgeaut', 'Smyrna', 'Champion' and 'Rea's Mammoth' can be relied upon. 'De Vranja' colours well and is resistant to fleck, a leaf-spotting fungus.

While apples and pears don't like damp soil, quinces are more tolerant but none of them likes very wet roots.

PRESERVING THE CROP

pears

STORING Ripen at room temperature then store in the refrigerator. Some pears don't change colour so don't use this as a guide to their ripeness.

FREEZING Pears can be chopped and frozen but used in cooked recipes only. Pears will exude their juice which has to be cooked off.

PICKLING Pears can be pickled with spices and vinegar. Pack into hot sterilised jars (see Bottling, page 118), seal while hot and store in a cool, dry place for up to 6 months. Once opened, store in the refrigerator.

for the table

to serve

～ Serve roasted APPLES stuffed with prunes and rosemary with roast pork.

～ Add julienne APPLES to a bitter salad of endive and a vinaigrette dressing.

～ Poach APPLES in a vanilla-scented syrup; serve with vanilla ice-cream.

～ Poached PEARS can be pan-fried in butter with honey. Serve warm or cold with caramel-flavoured cream or ice-cream.

～ A PEAR salad with mizuna and hazelnuts will benefit from the reinforcement of nut flavour found in a hazelnut oil vinaigrette.

～ QUINCES require long, slow cooking. Peel, slice and poach very gently in a sugar syrup for as little as 1 hour and up to 4–5 hours until the flesh has changed to a rich red or is soft. Store, covered in the refrigerator until required. Covered with sugar syrup, they will last for about a week.

quince and pistachio cake

This cake is delicious for afternoon tea or dessert. Try replacing the pistachios with toasted slivered almonds, if you like.

³/₄ cup (110g) caster sugar

¹/₂ cup (125ml) orange juice

1 cup (250ml) water

2 cardamom pods, crushed

3 medium quinces (990g), peeled, cored and sliced

PISTACHIO CAKE BATTER

90g butter

2 teaspoons grated orange rind

1 cup (220g) caster sugar

3 eggs

¹/₂ cup (75g) self-raising flour

1 cup (150g) plain flour

¹/₄ teaspoon bicarbonate of soda

¹/₂ cup (125ml) sour cream

¹/₄ cup (60ml) orange juice

¹/₂ cup (75g) chopped toasted pistachios

COMBINE SUGAR, juice, water and cardamom pods in a medium pan; stir over heat without boiling until sugar is dissolved. Add quinces; simmer, uncovered for about 1¹/₄ hours until quinces are soft and liquid almost absorbed; cool. Remove cardamom pods.

GREASE deep 22cm (8¹/₂") round cake pan; cover base with baking paper. Arrange two-thirds of the quince over the base of the pan. Blend the remaining quince until smooth. Gently fold quince puree into pistachio cake batter to give a rippled effect. Spread cake batter over quince in cake pan. Bake in moderate oven 1¹/₄ hours or until cooked when tested. Stand cake in pan for 15 minutes before turning onto a wire rack. Cake can be served hot or room temperature, with cream, custard or ice-cream.

PISTACHIO CAKE BATTER Beat butter, rind and sugar in large bowl with electric mixer until well combined and light. Beat in eggs, one at a time, until well combined. Stir in sifted flours and soda with combined cream and juice in two batches. Fold in pistachios.

Serves 8–10.

The cake can be made up to 3 days ahead, but is not suitable to freeze.

PRESERVING THE CROP

quinces

STORING Store in a cool, dry place for several weeks (for jelly or jam, don't store this long as the pectin reduces on storing).

FREEZING Blanched quince wedges can be frozen for up to 3 months (see Freezing, page 117). Best used frozen, not thawed.

PICKLING The ever-popular jelly or quince paste keeps almost indefinitely in an airtight container. Quinces can also be pickled (see Bottling, page 118).

PRESERVING THE CROP
kiwi fruit

STORING Kiwi fruit stores well at room temperature for up to a week. Store separately as the ethylene from other fruit (such as apples and bananas) ripens kiwi fruit before you need them. Once they give a little when pressed gently, store in the refrigerator for several days. Like melons, they are best served cool but not too cold.

FREEZING Kiwi fruit are not suitable to freeze.

PICKLING Jam and chutney can be made from kiwi fruit. They must be peeled before use. Spoon the hot jam or chutney into hot sterilised jars (see Bottling, page 118), and seal while still hot. Store for several months.

A refreshing sorbet can be made from kiwi fruit, but be careful to not over-process the seeds as they can leave an unpleasant fuzzy feeling in the mouth.

kiwi fruit
in the garden

Once these small, brown furry vine fruits were known as "Chinese gooseberries" until farmers in New Zealand discovered they excelled at growing them and bred new, improved varieties. They are now marketed worldwide as kiwi fruit and the "Chinese" name is all but gone. Their almost unbelievable bright green colour, soft flesh and sharp, sweet taste have become standard additions in fruit salads and desserts.

Kiwi fruit, with their downy coats, grow on an equally downy, deciduous vine that clambers upwards by twisting its strong stems around trellises, pergolas, verandah rails or through trees. A kiwi fruit vine can be a useful alternative to grapes as a summer sun shield and will allow winter sun through as the leaves drop.

For the best growth, kiwi fruit need a long warm summer and a cool, frost-free winter. Their roots are shallow and fibrous, so keep them well watered right through summer.

Spread a thick mulch of old manure, well-rotted compost or leaf mulch and the complete garden fertiliser of your choice each spring to protect the roots from drying out.

There are male and female plants so you must plant a pair for the spring blossoms to pollinate. If you want to plant more than a pair for extra fruit, one male plant can cope with five rapacious females.

The large, rough leaves shield the developing fruit from the sun during summer. In autumn as the leaves fall, the low sun sweetens the fruit. Pick them as you need them before they drop off the vine.

for the table
to serve...

∽ Kiwi fruit are high in vitamin C and are very convenient to serve. You only have to peel them. They can also be spooned out like boiled eggs.

∽ Kiwi fruit are best enjoyed as they are. They do not cook well but can have a flavoured syrup poured over them if you wish for something a little more exotic. Try an orange or mandarin-flavoured liqueur in the syrup.

∽ Kiwi fruit is high in enzymes and can be used as a meat tenderiser. Puree several kiwi fruit, add pepper and use as a marinade for meat. Leave for several hours, then discard the marinade and cook the meat as desired.

∽ Peel kiwi fruit and cut into wedges. Combine with passionfruit pulp and some orange-flavoured liqueur for an almost instant sauce.

melons

in the garden

These luscious summer and early autumn fruits are produced on a vine with leaves that are dry, leathery and prickly to touch. Their fruits are sweet and delicious with flesh in the most delightful range of colours: deep pink, soft orange, luminous limpid green or pale gold.

For general cultivation advice and soil preparation, see the sections on cucumbers and cucurbits on pages 42–43 and 54–55.

We are familiar with the more common varieties of melons, such as watermelons, rockmelons and honeydew. Watermelon varieties are now available in different sizes and some have reduced numbers of seeds. There are varieties with light pink or white flesh, and some with unusual skins like 'Moon and Stars'.

Rockmelons (or cantaloupes) also come in an assortment of shapes, skin colours and sizes. The honeydews come in a variety of colours: some green, some white-fleshed.

For truly unusual varieties, try specialist mail-order seed suppliers and companies that specialise in heritage seeds. You can also save seeds from last year's favourite crops, and friends are always happy to share seeds.

Whichever melon variety you choose, plant them as early as possible in spring after frosts have ceased as the fruits take about 4 months to mature. Follow the advice on pages 42–43 and 54–55 for soil care, spacing and seed planting. Nurseries will often carry seedlings. Each plant can comfortably support 4-5 melons, so cut back extra stems still growing once fruits have formed and break off any baby fruit in excess. This will result in good-sized, juicy melons.

A white patch on the skin of developing melons can indicate sunscald. If possible, wind some leafy stems over the fruit or erect a screen to protect the rest of the crop. They are ripe and ready to pick when fully expanded and firm.

for the table

to serve...

~ Melons have a great affinity with salty and spicy foods. Wrap pieces of melon in prosciutto as a finger food. It's a well-known combination but it never ceases to please.

~ Slices of well-chilled melon finish an Asian-inspired meal beautifully.

~ Try rockmelon drizzled with port. Vodka over watermelon adds a kick. Gin over honeydew melon is another great combination.

The three most popular melons: watermelon, rockmelon (cantaloupe) and honeydew.

PRESERVING THE CROP
melons

STORING Melons can be stored whole at room temperature for up to a week. When cut, press plastic wrap onto the cut surface and, for rockmelon, place in a sealed container or plastic bag to stop the aroma invading the fridge.

FREEZING Melons can be frozen in chunks (see Freezing, page 117), then pureed and served as a sorbet or water-ice.

PICKLING Use watermelon rind in pickles flavoured with cinnamon sticks and allspice. Pack into sterilised jars (see Bottling, page 118), seal while still hot and store in a cool, dry place for up to 6 months. Once opened, store in the refrigerator.

autumn herbs

PRESERVING THE CROP

rosemary

STORING Fresh is best, but home-dried rosemary (see Drying, page 119) keeps its flavour for longer than commercially dried rosemary. Store fresh stalks in a plastic bag in the refrigerator.

FREEZING Can be frozen for up to 6 months (see Freezing, page 117). There's no need to chop; freeze the stalks on a flat tray and, when frozen, transfer them to a plastic freezer bag, the needles will break off from the stems.

lemon grass

STORING The fresher the better, so leave in the garden as long as you can. If you must store fresh lemon grass, cut as little as possible from the stalks, leaving the root end intact, wrap in damp paper towel in a plastic bag, and store in the refrigerator for a couple of days only.

FREEZING Can be chopped and frozen in small batches (see Freezing, page 117). It will keep in the freezer for up to 6 months.

DRYING Dried lemon grass is integral to some Asian dishes but don't keep for longer than a couple of months or you will be disappointed in the taste (see Drying, page 119).

chillies

STORING Should be stored in a cool, dry place for up to a week. Pack loosely so air can circulate through them.

FREEZING Chopped fresh chillies can be frozen for about 6 months. Add them frozen to cooked dishes.

DRYING Thread chillies onto a thread or string and hang in an airy place to dry (see Drying, page 119). The heat intensifies on drying so use with caution.

The full range of spring and summer herbs is generally available through autumn, but here we pay particular attention to those herbs seemingly designed for the dishes we associate with cooler weather. Rosemary teams up with roasted meats and barbecues, while lemon grass and chilli, those essential ingredients in Asian curries and soups, add heat and piquancy. All three are easy to grow in the garden or in pots.

in the garden

rosemary

Rosemary is a tough shrub with thin, stiff, aromatic leaves or needles. Its basic form is stoutly upright and dense with pale mauve flowers at the stem tips during autumn and winter. Another variety is prostrate and drapes itself down walls or rocks, or spreads like a mat over the ground. Its flowers are sky-blue.

This plant likes a challenge: seaside sites, strong winds, dry rocky slopes, heavy snow or baking sun, and almost any type of soil. However, it won't survive soggy conditions and total shade. It is the ideal plant for pots and can be formal enough to look and smell impressive on a sunny doorstep or stand shoulder to shoulder with a line-up of potted herbs along a pathway.

When the plant is still small, nip a few leaves at a time until it starts to expand. It does take its time. Rosemary lasts many years, eventually becoming a sizeable shrub that will need repotting, seeing out successions of basil, chervil and parsley.

ABOVE Assorted chilli shapes
LEFT A gift for non-gardening chefs

lemon grass

Lemon grass is exactly that: a grass. It's perennial and forms a dramatic dense clump of tall, weeping foliage. It also makes a great tufted display in a large pot. Like other grasses, it is hardy as well. Try not to plant it too close to paths or steps as the leaves are sharp to brush against, although its scent is delightfully aromatic.

It grows best in full sun or just dappled shade in well-drained soil and tolerates tropical right through to temperate climates. It even tolerates a windy site. Give it a good soak around the roots every week in dry weather and provided you don't use every cane that develops, in time it will form a large clump. The leaves can be used fresh or dried as a tea but they will become ragged and rust-spotted during winter. You can either ignore its looks or cut it back to 15cm (6") above the ground, thus leaving the stems to use while the new leaves push through the centre and unfurl.

chillies

Chillies are related to capsicums and grow under the same conditions. See page 50–51 for details. Most develop into spreading sub-shrubs 1m (3') or more tall and wide in a season. Chillies flower in spring and summer and the chillies hang on the plants well into winter in mild gardens. Frosts and very cold winds will destroy them. You many be able to prune them down to 15cm (6") in autumn and in cool and cold zones protect with straw or compost and manure over winter. They will sprout again as the warm weather commences.

Seeds and seedlings are available from nurseries and dried seeds from varieties you have tried are often successful. The heat of chillies is generally rated 1 (mild) to 10 (hottest). Paprika is mild; Jalapeño is medium; Thai and Birdseye are hot; and the declared winner at 10 is Habanero.

for the table

to serve...

~ ROSEMARY sprigs added to a bottle of red wine vinegar along with a few peppercorns makes a beautiful salad dressing. For a smoky rosemary taste, add sprigs to the fire when barbecuing lamb or chicken.

~ When making sweet chilli dipping sauce for fresh spring rolls, delete some of the chilli and add chopped fresh LEMON GRASS instead. Use lemon grass as giant skewers for chicken and pork. Quarter the stalks before threading meat cubes onto them; cook on a ridged grill pan or barbecue.

~ Wear disposable gloves when preparing CHILLIES and scrub the chopping board well. Always wash your hands after handling chillies. For chilli-flavoured oil, heat 12 small fresh chillies in peanut oil until warm but not hot. Remove from heat and steep at room temperature for 2 hours. Drain the oil into hot, sterilised bottles (see Bottling, page 118) and seal while the bottle is still hot. Store at room temperature for up to 6 months or refrigerate.

chilli coriander jam

It does not matter how much you make, everyone always wants more!

8 large tomatoes (2kg), cored

2/3 cup (160ml) olive oil

10 cloves garlic, peeled

1 tablespoon grated fresh ginger

10 small fresh red chillies, stems removed

2 tablespoons cumin seeds

2 tablespoons black mustard seeds

3/4 cup (180ml) red wine vinegar

1/4 cup (60ml) nam pla (Thai fish sauce)

1 1/4 cups (335g) palm sugar, chopped

1 tablespoon ground turmeric

1/2 cup chopped fresh coriander leaves and roots

RUB TOMATOES with olive oil; place in a roasting pan and cook in a moderate oven for about 30 minutes or until soft but not coloured.

PROCESS GARLIC, ginger, chillies, cumin and mustard seeds in a food processor until chopped and well combined. Transfer mixture to a large heavy-based pan, add tomatoes, vinegar, nam pla, sugar and turmeric; simmer for about 2 hours or until thick and jammy. Process in batches until combined but still textured. Return to heat for 5 minutes or until hot; stir in coriander. Spoon into hot sterilised jars; seal while hot.

Makes about 6 cups (1 1/2 litres).

Store in cool dry place for up to 6 months. Once opened, refrigerate.

Winter

USE BAY LEAVES FRESH OR DRIED

Winter garden diary

There are two schools of thought on winter.

There are those people who dread it, hide away and grizzle about the cold air, the clothing layers, the dampness that seems to cling to everything and the cost of heating.

There are those who relish the battle that nature thrusts their way, the extra energy and "go" that cool air engenders, the brilliance of sunlit days or the haze of cloudy ones, and long cook-ups in the kitchen.

For some in the tropics, winter is pure heaven with dry, balmy days and cool breezes at night. The subtropics see cool mornings and evenings, with wintry days interspersed with sunny ones. Cool weather is deemed an inconvenient disruption. Those in cold zones rug up to go outside, and those with inefficient heating rug up to stay inside.

And gardeners everywhere busy themselves with what they consider to be the season's appropriate business.

In cold zones there'll be scurries out to harvest fresh offerings and a prowl around to view the cold and wind-wracked berries and skeletonised flower tops, and to look for signs of spring. Indoors, there will be growers' lists and seed catalogues to peruse and some early seedling trays to establish to get things started early.

The Mediterranean wet season will be flattening all in its path, and the longed-for rain will be soaking through the soil layers. The sound of roots, stems and leaves refilling is almost audible and plants start to stand up proud again until a polar blast makes them reconsider. In protected sites where water does not pool, there will be vegetables and herbs aplenty, and maintenance tasks to match.

In contrast, in subtropical areas, gardeners need to be wary of drying winds. The sun is not as hot as in summer but if the signs are ignored, plants will die. There'll be supplies of winter vegetables and herbs, and little insect damage.

In the tropics, winter is perhaps the busiest season. Fast-growing crops need trimming and feeding, vines need controlling, and the soil cries out for revitalising in preparation for the series of replacement crops that warm conditions will allow.

So let's view the winter garden bounty.

pick now...

COOL CONTINENTAL, TEMPERATE AND MEDITERRANEAN GARDENS WITH FREQUENT FROSTS

- beetroot
- broad beans
- broccoli
- Brussels sprouts
- cabbage
- cauliflower
- lettuce with protection
- mushrooms
- spinach with protection
- swede
- turnip

TEMPERATE, MEDITERRANEAN AND SUBTROPICAL GARDENS WITH NO FROSTS

- Asian greens
- carrots
- endive
- mizuna
- peas
- rocket
- plus all the above with no protection

TROPICAL GARDENS

- beans
- capsicum
- corn
- cucumber
- eggplant
- tomatoes
- zucchini
- plus all the above except Brussels sprouts

plant now...

COLD ZONES WITH FROST, PLANT UNDER GLASS ON HEATED TRAYS OR IN THE HOUSE TOWARDS THE END OF WINTER

- capsicum
- chillies
- corn
- cucumbers
- eggplant
- lettuce
- melons
- squash
- tomatoes

FROST-FREE ZONES

- broad beans
- beetroot
- cabbage
- lettuce and salad greens
- peas
- potatoes
- silverbeet
- spinach
- plus all the above

TROPICAL GARDENS

- beans
- plus all of the above

CLOCKWISE FROM TOP LEFT Palm leaf kale, or Italian cabbage, is a stunning colour and can be cut leaf by leaf; Pusstopher relaxes during the harvest; a bowl of white-stemmed bok choy, bouquet-like tat soi and leafy choy sum; to preserve such rustic treasures, rub them with linseed oil; garden colour and delight is supplied by blue kale.

the brassicas

The beautiful blue–grey colouring of these brassicas looks majestic with the crumpled green of silverbeet.

The brassicas, better known as the cabbage group of vegetables, are the stalwarts of winter. Rounded, florid, bulbous and possessed of wonderful foliage colours from silver, grey-green, yellow to bright green, these over-sized and baroque-looking vegetables make striking crops when the winter garden beds might otherwise be bare.

Brassicas actually prefer the cold conditions of winter and are not much pleased by hot temperatures and the baking sun. They make ideal home crops during that time of the year when the garden has withdrawn for winter and gardeners themselves prefer the great indoors.

The brassica family is a large one and includes cabbages, cauliflower, broccoli, Brussels sprouts and kale. These are the slow-growing members of the tribe that can take anywhere between 3–5 months to be ready to pick.

Also part of the brassica family are the quick-growing Asian greens that have had such an culinary impact in the West over recent years. Bok choy (Chinese chard), tat soi (Chinese flat cabbage) and choy sum (Chinese flowering cabbage) are ready to harvest in 6–8 weeks. The salad feathers of mizuna are the speed champions with early leaves harvestable in 20 days.

Over the following pages we feature the most common brassicas grown in home gardens. The fast-growing Asian greens are ideal for staggered planting and harvesting to ensure a steady supply for quick stir-fries and winter salads. The slow-growing brassicas are tantalising to watch as they solidly progress, their majestic leaves unfurl and their large, tightly-packed hearts and flower buds form.

general cultivation

Like all leafy crops, brassicas do best in soil that has been well-manured a month prior to planting to make it light and full of organic matter. Two weeks before planting, add a generous supply of nitrogen-rich fertiliser and a sprinkling of lime so all their required trace elements will be available from the soil.

If you haven't room to spare for a month of growing nothing, brassicas can be planted as a follow-on to beans, and they'll make use of the nitrogen stored in the bean roots. However, the seedlings will still need extra fertiliser and lime to boost them along.

The fast-growing brassicas are usually planted from seed *in situ* or in seed trays, and can be harvested and thinned as they develop.

The slow-growers are usually raised in seedling trays or shallow pots, or bought as seedlings and planted out when the soil is ready. This gives them a head start and allows their roots to become firmly established.

If wanting to raise crops from seed, cover the seeds with 0.5cm ($^1/_4$") of sand or seed-raising mixture. They'll emerge in 6–10 days with 2 almost heart-shaped leaves. Once they've developed their miniature, true leaves, thin them in the garden or plant out seedlings 50–75cm (20–30") apart for the slow-growers, 10–15cm (4–6") for the speedsters. Firm them in well.

Brassicas must be planted in full sun with well-drained soil to reduce the risk of fungal problems. It's often a good idea to raise the soil into mounds or furrows and plant the seedlings on the top. Always keep well watered. Irrigation by means of the furrows is preferable to overhead waterings.

pests and diseases

The whole brassica family is the mainstay in the life cycle of the cabbage moth and the cabbage white butterfly, both of which deposit their eggs on the leaves. The leaves are then consumed by the developing caterpillars. The leaf surfaces are eaten first, then whole sections of leaf. The cabbage moth caterpillar will even eat right into the heart of the cabbage.

Pick the caterpillars off by hand as soon as you see them or spray with an insecticide. See page 9 for non-chemical sprays and organic alternatives.

Aphids can gather among the grey foliage, and weaken the plant as they suck out its nourishment. Keep alert for mass attacks and pick off, hose off or spray. Again, see page 9 for non-chemical treatments.

PHOTO: SCOTT CAMERON

CABBAGE MOTH DAMAGE

CLUSTER OF BROCCOLI IN A NEST
OF LEAVES

broccoli

What can be more fetching to a gardening cook than a bouquet of broccoli? And that's exactly what a head of broccoli is: a cluster of buds harvested from the centre of rich blue–green leaves.

in the garden

For general soil preparation and cultivation notes, see page 97.

Broccoli grows best when the weather is cool, and will develop strongly and be more resistant to insect attack if given liquid fertiliser every 2–3 weeks.

Its bouquet of tight buds is produced in 3–4 months at the top of the stem. Always cut broccoli early when the buds are still tightly furled, and coloured either purplish or green, depending on the variety. If left too long before harvesting, the buds start to open and the flavour and texture change. Stems with yellow flowers form.

After the initial harvest, each plant starts to produce small stem offshoots of useful broccoli for another month or two. These small broccoli shoots are harvestable and good to eat. However, if any of the florets are allowed to ripen to yellow and open, the plant is satisfied it has run its course and will start to fade. So, for the longest possible harvest, keep trimming the side shoots until they become too small.

Some broccoli varieties have been specially bred to grow during warm weather so plant these for an early autumn crop.

'Romanesco' is a recently developed variety that has a limey-green flowerhead with tightly spiralled cones. It is sweetly flavoured and dramatic to serve whole but it behaves more like cauliflower in that it does not produce successive shoots.

for the table

to prepare...

~ Aphids, bugs and caterpillars love to hide in the florets of broccoli so soak for a short time in cold water and shake gently to release unwanted dinner guests.

~ Broccoli can be boiled, steamed, stir-fried or microwaved. Cut the florets from the stalk and use separately. Covering broccoli while cooking will preserve a stronger flavour.

~ The stems are edible, but need to have their tough outer skin removed before using raw in salads or tossing in a stir-fry (avoid over-cooking).

~ Try saving the stems and cook all at once in an Asian-style oyster sauce.

PRESERVING THE CROP

STORING Store in a vegetable storage bag in the refrigerator for up to 3 days. It's also possible to store broccoli, with stems in a container of water, in a vegetable storage bag for about 5 days.

FREEZING Broccoli can be blanched and frozen for several months. Pack into rigid containers and cook when needed in boiling water, unthawed (see Freezing, page 117). Cooked and pureed broccoli freezes very well for several months.

to serve...

∽ Use broccoli florets to carry strong flavours such as garlic and lemon. Use only lemon rind as the acid from the juice darkens and wrinkles the broccoli stems.

∽ Dotted with anchovy butter, steamed broccoli becomes a great accompaniment to a simple meal.

∽ Toss broccoli florets with brown butter and toasted almonds.

∽ Add finely chopped broccoli to a pasta sauce of Italian sausage and lots of garlic.

∽ Broccoli makes fantastic soup. Cook in chicken stock with fresh herbs and garlic, puree and add a dash of cream for a very elegant starter.

PHOTO: AWW HOME LIBRARY

crepes with creamy broccoli

1/3 cup (50g) wholemeal plain flour

2 tablespoons white self-raising flour

2 eggs, beaten lightly

2/3 cup (160ml) milk

1 tablespoon vegetable oil

1/4 cup (20g) grated parmesan cheese

BROCCOLI FILLING

750g broccoli, chopped

30g butter

2 green onions, chopped

1 tablespoon wholemeal plain flour

1/2 cup (125ml) milk

1/2 cup (125ml) cream

pinch ground nutmeg

COMBINE flours in a large bowl, gradually stir in combined eggs, milk and oil; mix to a smooth batter (or blend or process ingredients until smooth). Cover, stand 30 minutes.

POUR 1/4 cup of batter into heated greased heavy-based pan; cook crepe until lightly browned underneath. Turn crepe; brown on other side. Repeat with remaining batter. You will need 8 crepes for this recipe.

DIVIDE filling between crepes; fold crepes into triangles.

PLACE crepes in lightly greased ovenproof dish; sprinkle with cheese. Bake crepes in moderate oven about 10 minutes or until hot.

BROCCOLI FILLING Boil, steam or microwave broccoli until tender; drain. Heat butter in medium pan; cook onion, stirring, over medium heat 1 minute. Stir in flour; cook, stirring, over medium heat 1 minute. Remove from heat; gradually stir in combined milk, cream and nutmeg; stir over high heat until mixture boils and thickens. Stir in broccoli.

Serves 4.

Crepes and filling can be made a day ahead; keep covered in refrigerator.

PHOTO: THE DIGGER'S CLUB

CAULIFLOWERS WRAPPED IN THEIR EDIBLE LEAVES

cauliflower

Here's another flower-bud head that is prized when it's densely packed and its "curds", just like fresh cheese, are pure in colour and firm. As a gardening cook, you can assess the right moment to harvest. Straight from the garden, the cauliflower will break apart with a snap. Cauliflower is always less odorous when cooked fresh.

in the garden

For general soil preparation and cultivation notes, see page 97.

Cauliflowers are the fussiest of the brassicas to grow. They are very sensitive to soil pH. Diseases (such as club root) and deformed growth (whiptail) are caused by soil that is too acidic. Always add a generous handful of garden lime to each square metre (square yard) of soil when preparing the garden beds 2 weeks before planting. Sprinkle another dusting of lime over the soil 1 week after the seedlings have been planted.

Cauliflowers are generally ready to harvest in 4–6 months and need cool temperatures and full sun to grow well. Start to raise seeds in early or mid-summer so you can plant them before summer's end. Seedlings are also available from nurseries. Plant them out 60–80cm (24–32") apart.

The young cauliflower plants need to be well established by the time winter begins as the cool weather is essential for the cauliflower heads to develop. In the heat of summer the heads start to open and break up.

As the heads form, protect them from the sun by tying their large leaves into a teepee above or breaking them and folding over the white heads. The heads will yellow if exposed to the sun. The leaves of some varieties grow around the head and automatically shelter it.

Peep regularly under their covers to watch for when the flowers become tight and solid. Harvest them straight away or they'll open out.

Unlike broccoli, cauliflowers put their all into one flower, so there is no repeat harvest. It is a good idea when planting the seedlings to hold a few back and plant 2–3 weeks later to stagger the crop.

Several white cauliflower varieties are available and differ only in the length of time they take to form. 'Alverda' is a variety with greenish curds. Pink, green, purple and even orange varieties are available in Europe. Their flavours are as individual as their colourings.

Mini cauliflowers are formed by planting seedlings only 25–30cm (10–12") apart and harvesting the small heads as soon as they reach 10cm (4") across, in about 4 months. Keep up follow-on plantings as the cauliflowers are harvested one by one.

PRESERVING THE CROP

STORING Cover the cauliflower with paper towel before storing in a vegetable storage bag in the refrigerator for up to a week.

FREEZING Cauliflower can be blanched and frozen (see Freezing, page 117) for up to 4 months. Store in rigid containers so the florets do not break up.

for the table

to prepare...

⌇ Soak the florets in cold water for a short period before cooking to flush out any bugs or caterpillars.

⌇ Cauliflower can be boiled, steamed, stir-fried or microwaved.

to serve...

⌇ For a delicious soup, cook cauliflower in a strong chicken stock with onions; blend, adding some fresh dill sprigs. Return to heat and warm through, adding enough cream to make a thick but smooth soup.

⌇ Steam cauliflower and top with crisped chopped bacon, toasted breadcrumbs and a drizzle of butter; brown under a hot grill.

⌇ Add cauliflower to a salad of red and yellow capsicum, tomatoes and strips of crisped salami. Toss with Italian dressing.

⌇ Cauliflower cheese is an age-old favourite. Any leftovers can be blended until smooth and thinned with a little milk to make an instant soup.

piccalilli

Cauliflower pickles are a great way to preserve cauliflower (you can also include carrots, celery, green tomatoes, cucumber and pickling onions in varying amounts).

1 kg vegetables
4 cups (1 litre) white vinegar
1 cup (220g) sugar
1 tablespoon ground turmeric
1 tablespoon mustard powder
3 cloves garlic, sliced
4 small red Thai chillies, halved lengthways
1/3 cup (75g) cornflour

SALT THE VEGETABLES OVERNIGHT and rinse well in cold water the following morning, drain well.

COMBINE vinegar with the sugar, turmeric, mustard powder, garlic and chilli. Bring to boil, add vegetables, cover and simmer for about 5 minutes or until the vegetables are just tender.

TAKE 1/2 cup (125ml) of liquid from the pan and blend with cornflour. Stir into pan return to the boil until thickened; about 3 minutes. Pour into hot sterilised jars and seal while hot (see Bottling, page 118). Store in a cool, dry place for 4 weeks before using. Once opened, store in the refrigerator.

Cabbages framed by beans, sweet corn and silverbeet run to seed.

cabbage & brussels sprouts

Perhaps not the most glamorous duo in the brassica folio, cabbages and and Brussels sprouts are both stout winter growers and can be extremely attractive and a reason for pride in the garden. They are also just as attractive on the table.

in the garden

For general soil preparation and cultivation notes, see page 97.

cabbage

Of all the brassicas, cabbages are the most tolerant of warm conditions. There are varieties that can be planted to provide a continuous harvest right through the year in most climates. Cabbages can be picked small or left to become full-sized but their holding ability is better in cooler weather. They start to crack open, even rot, if left too long.

In cold climates, ensure autumn seedlings are solidly established before the frosts arrive and in the tropics, plant seedlings in time for them to mature in the dry rather than the wet.

There are an astounding number of varieties. There are those with conical heads such as 'Sugarloaf' or 'Durham Early' which are quick maturing for speedy, warm-weather crops. Others develop tight, round heads and varieties include the fast-growing minis and 'Earliball' and the larger, slower winter regulars like 'January King' (for the English winter) and 'Primo'. Colours vary from deep to light green, grey, purple-green and rich beet red. Leaf textures offer more variety with some tightly stretched and smooth around the head and others rumpled and creased as in the 'Savoy' cabbages.

Then there are the kales which are loose-leaf cabbages. The leaves fan out in the same manner as spinach and Swiss chard. Their young leaves and also the older leaves, though strongly flavoured, can be cooked. They are particularly suited to stir-frying. There are plain-leafed varieties that can stand nearly 1m (3') tall like 'Cottages' and 'Chou Moellier'. Others are curly and fringed like the 'Scotch', 'Tall Green Curled' and 'Ornamental'. Palm tree kale, or Italian cabbage, has dark grey, crumpled leaves.

Experiment with cabbage varieties that you have never tried before. Certainly choose according to culinary desires, but also be adventurous and use cabbages as ornamental winter garden features for there are few vegetables as showy and dramatic. You'll be rewarded with a wintertime chorus of cabbage leaf shapes and colours, all with a sweet cabbage flavour.

brussels sprouts

If you can't provide a long, cool winter, it's best not to try to grow Brussels sprouts. They grow in the same manner as their brassica relatives but develop a tall, strong stem. Feed regularly with liquid fertiliser and hill up the soil around the stem base to support it. The more leaves that develop up the stem, the more sprouts you'll be able to gather from the leaf junctions.

As the sprouts start to form near the base, strip the lowers leaves from the stem with a sideways pull so the sprouts can develop round and firm. You'll be able to harvest in 4–5 months.

Gather the sprouts as they develop, or cut the stem at the growing point when it's about 40cm (16") tall and they'll all mature at once. Discard those sprouts that start to burst open; the ideal sprout is tightly furled and about 5cm (2") in diameter.

As soon as the buds start to form, remember to spread around a slug and snail deterrent as both of them relish such new morsels.

for the table

to prepare...

⟿ Cabbage and Brussels sprouts can be boiled, steamed, microwaved or eaten raw. Avoid adding large amounts of cooking water. Rinse cabbage, shake off excess water and cook, covered. Never overcook either of these vegetables as the smell and taste becomes unpalatable.

to serve...

⟿ Sprinkle CABBAGE generously with crisp chopped pancetta, garlic and a little butter.

⟿ Finely shred CABBAGE and add to a pan of boiling water with a spoonful of caraway seeds; return to the boil. Remove from the heat; drain and add a knob of butter before serving.

⟿ Stir-fry shredded CABBAGE until crisp; drizzle with sesame oil and sprinkle with sesame seeds. Great tossed through noodles.

⟿ Finely shredded CABBAGE also shines, raw, as a salad. Shred or grate carrots and peppers; toss with mung bean sprouts and a chilli-flavoured vinaigrette for a new-look coleslaw. A packet of fried noodles added just before serving adds crunch.

⟿ BRUSSELS SPROUTS, steamed lightly, then tossed in a hot pan with olive oil and fresh chestnuts will accompany a grilled steak perfectly.

⟿ Toss halved BRUSSELS SPROUTS in melted butter. Add some white wine and chicken stock and a handful of sultanas. Cook, covered, until sprouts are soft, remove lid and cook until liquid is almost absorbed. Serve with grilled or roasted meats.

PRESERVING THE CROP

STORING Cabbages are best stored whole in the refrigerator. Once cut, they should be used within a few days. Brussels sprouts can be stored in a vegetable storage bag for several days in the refrigerator.

FREEZING Cabbage can be shredded and blanched, then frozen for up to 6 months; cook from frozen. Brussels sprouts can be blanched and frozen for up to 6 months in rigid containers to keep their shape (see Freezing, page 117).

PICKLING Pickled red cabbage is popular. Salt the cabbage and stand overnight; rinse well the following day. Pack the cabbage into hot sterilised jars (see Bottling, page 118). Heat white vinegar with sugar and spices, such as cloves and cinnamon, until boiling and pour over cabbage in jars; seal while hot.

Steaming retains the brilliant colour of Brussels sprouts.

asian greens

PHOTOS: AWW HOME LIBRARY

PRESERVING THE CROP

STORING Store all Asian greens in vegetable storage bags in the refrigerator for 1–2 days only. Wong nga bok (Chinese cabbage) will last for longer if stored whole. Once cut, use as quickly as possible.

FREEZING These vegetables don't survive the freezing process well.

CHOY SUM

GAI LARN

TAT SOI

Asian greens are the speedsters of the brassica family. They all grow very quickly and are best cooked rapidly to preserve their brilliant green colouring, as it's their stems and leaves that we relish. They are the soft and juicy members of the brassica troupe and many have a deliciously sharp flavour.

in the garden

Asian greens grow fast and succulent only if hurried along. Start with rich soil and add weekly applications of liquid fertiliser so that their stems and leaves don't become stringy. Frequent water keeps them bulky. Flood the root zone every 3–4 days if the weather is dry and test the soil with your finger after rain to make sure moisture has gone through to the roots. Often the large leaves deflect light showers. Asian greens don't tolerate frosts, but will grow year-round in frost-free areas and the tropics.

In very small gardens, grow varieties you can harvest leaf by leaf, and plant replacement crops every 2 weeks or so. Move the brassica site every 6 months to deter insects, prevent the build-up of soil diseases and to rest the soil.

A shallow, 30–40 cm (12–16") pot filled with very rich potting mix will support a selection of strongly flavoured greens and lettuce for a garden salad mix. It must be in full sun and well watered. Your "salad bowl" will last a month or two, and so plant a second pot 3–4 weeks after the original.

GAI LARN (Chinese broccoli) has long, slender stems, large leaves and a small bud or white flower cluster. When the buds are closed, they are edible but should be removed if open. They can be picked in 8–10 weeks.

BOK CHOY (Chinese chard, also pak choi, senposai and baby bok choy) has heavy white stems the same length as its leaves. It takes 5–6 weeks to grow but the odd leaf can be used while it's developing.

GAI CHOY (mustard cabbage) is more leaf than stem and is ready in 6–8 weeks, odd leaves being available as they grow. When full size, cut off at the roots and cook whole.

TAT SOI (Chinese flat cabbage, rosette bok choy, also komatsuma) forms an open cluster of deep green leaves with brilliant white stems. It spreads out to 30cm (12") like a glorious green posy. Use leaf by leaf or cut off whole. It has a slightly strong flavour and is ready to harvest in 8 weeks.

WONG NGA BOK (Chinese cabbage) is a tall, elongated cabbage, lighter and less tightly packed, and develops its fully enwrapped form in 8–10 weeks.

CHOY SUM (Chinese flowering cabbage) is very similar to Chinese broccoli with long stems, rounded leaves and a small bud or yellow flower cluster. Again, the closed buds are edible while the open buds are not. They can be picked in 8–10 weeks.

MIZUNA, another of the brassicas, is described on page 45.

pests and diseases

Asian greens are prone to the same cabbage moth and butterfly caterpillar attacks as the slow-growing brassicas but their faster growth makes damage less likely. Slugs and snails love the lush, new growth, so protect seedlings as they emerge and keep renewing the baits as the plants develop. See page 9 for alternative deterrents or baits.

for the table

to prepare...

Harvest all Asian greens as close to preparation as possible. Pick whole or pick only as much as you need and only wash when ready to prepare.

Harvest choy sum (Chinese flowering cabbage) and gai larn (Chinese broccoli) as the flowers open and while many buds are still tightly furled.

to serve...

CHOY SUM (Chinese flowering cabbage) can be lightly boiled, steamed or microwaved and served with any traditional butter sauce such as hollandaise. It's traditionally served with oyster sauce.

BOK CHOY AND BABY BOK CHOY (Chinese chard) can be boiled, steamed, stir-fried or microwaved. Add pancetta, garlic and parmesan or stir-fry with garlic and serve with sesame oil and a sprinkling of sesame seeds.

WONG NGA BOK (Chinese cabbage) can be used in the same way as for European cabbage and is great raw in salads. Stuff the leaves with a pork mince and rice vermicelli filling and steam; drizzle with soy sauce mixed with rice wine just before serving.

TAT SOI (Chinese flat cabbage) can be used in the same way as bok choy or wong nga bok. Add raw to salads but remember it has a stronger flavour than the bok choy we're used to.

GAI LARN (Chinese broccoli) needs the tough outer stem layer removed before cooking. Cook the stems first and add the chopped leaves towards the end. Great with a little butter and salt and pepper, and it's also good with pork or chicken in the Asian way.

GAI CHOY (mustard cabbage) can be added whole to soups; it is great with rich meats such as duck and pork. It can be bought preserved in Asian supermarkets and should be rinsed before using. Deep-fry leaves until translucent and use as a bed for fish and seafood.

PHOTO: AWW HOME LIBRARY

bok choy steamed with chilli oil

4 baby bok choy (600g)
1 tablespoon peanut oil
2 cloves garlic, crushed
2 tablespoons light soy sauce
1 1/2 teaspoons hot chilli sauce
2 green onions, sliced
1/4 cup fresh coriander leaves
1 small red Thai chilli, seeded, sliced thinly

HALVE bok choy lengthways; place, cut-side up, in bamboo steamer, drizzle with combined oil, garlic and sauces.

STEAM bok choy, covered, over wok or large saucepan of simmering water about 5 minutes or until just tender. Serve bok choy sprinkled with onion, coriander and chilli.

Serves 4.

mushrooms

PINHEADS TURN TO BUTTONS OVERNIGHT

PRESERVING THE CROP

STORING Never store mushrooms in a plastic bag. Paper bags are great; a plain cotton drawstring bag, used just for this purpose, is wonderful. Store in paper or cloth in the refrigerator.

FREEZING Mushrooms can be frozen whole (for buttons) for about a month if raw, or sauté in butter and they can be frozen for about 3 months. Add these mushrooms whole to casseroles as they go a little soggy. Soup of pureed mushrooms can be frozen for up to 3 months (see Freezing, page 117).

DRYING Mushrooms can be dried in paper bags in an airy position (see Drying, page 119).

PICKLING If you've a glut of mushrooms, try pickling them whole and using as finger food or on antipasto platters (see recipe, opposite).

With their softly furred white skins and brown–grey gills, mushrooms are invitingly tactile and very ornamental. Their aroma is clean and earthy and their flavour follows suit. In all honesty, however, we can't claim that mushrooms are a garden crop. The mushroom we recognise, harvest and appreciate is the fruiting body, the seed or (more accurately) the spore-releaser of the underground system – which is the real "plant".

Harvesting wild mushrooms can be dangerous for the uninitiated as not all mushrooms are edible so, in a word, don't. It's much tamer, and safer, to raise mushrooms from a kit. While not exactly a garden crop, mushrooms are a fascinating form of life and very easy to grow once you've opened the box and watered the compost mix.

in the garden

Mushroom kits are readily available from nurseries and produce stores. They consist of two packages of compost material, one of which contains the thread-like vegetative part of mushrooms called the mycelium. This layer is dampened to activate its growth and, after a week, is combined with the second bag of mix.

The container is stored in a dark, cool position as the fungi won't "fruit" if they're too hot or too light. Mushrooms like temperatures around 12–18°C (55–65°F), and storage in a cupboard, shady shed or cellar is ideal. Choose a spot with easy access for checking and harvesting.

The first pinheads will appear within 14–20 days. The mushrooms develop quickly, from small specks to recognisable button forms overnight and full-blown mushrooms the following day. Harvest them as soon as they reach a suitable size and thus avoid overcrowding. Use a knife to make clean cuts and to disturb the mass as little as possible.

Several flushes of mushrooms will continue for a month or two, but eventually the mycelium is exhausted. If no fresh mushrooms develop after 21 days, consider the season over. Add the compost to the garden where its final performance will be helping other plants to grow.

Wild mushrooms are an autumnal treasure and there are avid bands of the cognoscenti who know what to gather and where. You often see groups combing fields and forests after the rain. You may be lucky enough to be invited to join a group or go to classes.

But it must be stressed that ill-informed wild mushroom gathering is nothing but dangerous.

for the table

to prepare...

⤳ Cultivated mushrooms are harvested and eaten at three different stages: buttons (still joined to the stems), cups (larger than buttons but with caps still closed), flat (fully open but still firm).

⤳ Cultivated mushrooms need no washing. If they have a covering of compost, brush gently with a damp piece of paper towel.

to serve...

⤳ For perfect breakfast mushrooms, sauté sliced cups in a little butter and oil until they have released their liquid, stir over high heat until liquid evaporates; sprinkle with a good quantity of lemon juice and chopped fresh parsley.

⤳ Flat mushrooms beg to be filled. Stuff with minced pork, water chestnuts and Asian flavourings; pan-fry until filling is cooked through.

⤳ Button mushrooms are great when dipped in a thin batter and deep-fried; serve with a very lemony herb mayonnaise.

⤳ For an easy pâté, cook chopped mushrooms with thyme, green onions and garlic; combine with cream cheese and a little cream. Press mixture into a loaf pan lined with plastic wrap; cover and refrigerate until firm. When firm, roll in chopped fresh parsley and serve with crackers.

mushrooms with bite

These are great as an appetiser or served alongside strong cheese as in a ploughman's lunch. Cup mushrooms can be used for this recipe but they may need to be quartered.

3 cups (750ml) cider vinegar

1/2 cup (125ml) lemon juice

10 whole white peppercorns

2 fresh bay leaves

2 sprigs fresh thyme

2 cloves garlic, thinly sliced

3 small fresh red Thai chillies, seeded

1kg button mushrooms

COMBINE ALL INGREDIENTS, except mushrooms, in a large pan. Bring to boil, reduce heat and simmer, covered, for 10 minutes.

ADD MUSHROOMS to pan and simmer uncovered for 10 minutes.

POUR mushrooms and cooking liquid into hot sterilised jars and seal while hot (see Bottling, page 118). Store in a cool, dry place for up to 6 months; refrigerate once opened.

spinach & silverbeet

STUNNING RUBY CHARD

These two leafy greens are often confused. Silverbeet is related to beetroot. It grows in a clump and its leaves are a thing of beauty: tall white stems with deep green, crinkly leaves that grow to 30–40cm (12–16"). Spinach, on the other hand, stands not quite so tall, has thin stems with clear, green leaves and a delicate, subtle taste.

in the garden

Both spinach and silverbeet require well-prepared soil. Dig in plenty of chicken manure and well-matured compost, with a dressing of nitrogen-rich fertiliser 2–3 weeks before planting in a sunny or lightly shaded spot with morning sun. Silverbeet prefers full sun. It performs best in the garden as it develops a large root system, but if grown in pots, silverbeet needs replacing often.

silverbeet

Silverbeet or chard seeds benefit from a soak in cold water for a few hours. Push the softened seeds down to the first finger joint, spacing them 30–40cm (12–16") apart. Stems and leaves will appear in 2 weeks. They may need thinning as several can emerge from each seed. Mulch and keep well watered. Give liquid feeds every 2 weeks in the cool of the day as fertiliser can burn in sunlight.

Harvest silverbeet leaves by breaking off outside leaves with a downward and sideways pull. Always keep 4–5 leaves in the centre. Break off any flower stems that start to form but when this happens prepare new seeds and garden beds as the end of the existing plants is nigh.

Silverbeet grows happily in most climates all year, though it displays a distinct preference for cool weather as it tends to run to seed in the heat and suffers rust spotting in humid conditions. In ideal conditions silverbeet keeps producing new leaves for almost a year and the stem will end up looking like a trunk. It's the ideal cut-and-come-again vegetable.

There is a variety of silverbeet known as perpetual spinach that is beautifully leafy and fine-stemmed. It grows very well in a pot as well as in the garden. Don't be deluded by the name "perpetual", however; it will need replacing in 3–6 months, especially if grown in a pot.

PRESERVING THE CROP

STORING Do not wash before storing. Place in a vegetable storage bag in the refrigerator for about 3 days.

FREEZING Both silverbeet and spinach can be blanched and frozen (see Freezing, page 117) for up to 6 months. On thawing you will need to squeeze out all the moisture and they will only be useful in cooked dishes such as pies, soups and casseroles.

Coloured "rainbow" forms are available with yellow, orange, red and pink stem colours, and ruby chard with red stems alone. They are stunning in the garden and add drama to the dinner plate.

spinach

When planting spinach seeds, position them 1cm (¹/₂") deep and 15cm (6") apart if planning to harvest leaf by leaf, and 20–30cm (8–12") apart for whole-plant harvesting. Closely planted seedlings can be thinned out later. They'll sprout in 2–3 weeks. Mulch well to keep their roots moist and cool and to suppress weeds.

Keep regularly watered and give boosts of liquid fertiliser every month. Both silverbeet and spinach also need mulch protection from frosts. You'll be able to pick the outside leaves in about 8 weeks.

Spinach is an easy, cool-season crop and is happy planted in pots, in clusters or in regimental rows. It grows best during the short days of winter. Spinach can either be harvested leaf by leaf, or pulled out whole, roots and all. Another method is to cut it off above the soil and the remaining root will obligingly re-shoot to produce a second crop, making it doubly worthwhile.

New Zealand spinach is a wild green that grows naturally along the coast in both Australia and New Zealand. It is also available as seed and will grow anywhere during the warm months and is most lush when given adequate water. The leaves grow on lanky stems which are fleshy and mildly flavoured. Harvest a length of stem and strip off the leaves.

for the table

to prepare...

◄ Wash well before using to remove dirt and grit. Wash in a sink of cold water, let the leaves float to the top and then scoop them out. Don't simply let the water drain away as this tends to re-coat the leaves in their grit.

to serve...

◄ Silverbeet and spinach can be used interchangeably but silverbeet has a stronger flavour and carries stronger flavours well.

◄ Mix SILVERBEET, fetta and pine nuts for seasoning a boned leg of lamb.

◄ The stems of SILVERBEET can be used as a dish on their own. Serve with a strong cheese sauce (with plenty of powdered mustard) and a gratin top.

◄ Add SPINACH by the handful to a risotto in the last moments of cooking.

◄ Combine SPINACH with ricotta to flavour gnocchi in a rich, cheesy sauce.

◄ Use both SPINACH and SILVERBEET leaves to wrap a filling of minced chicken and almonds, before steaming.

◄ Deep-fry shredded SILVERBEET and dress with a soy and rice wine dressing with lots of fried garlic, sesame seeds and a tiny sprinkle of sugar.

spinach soup with fetta

40g butter

1 medium brown onion (150g), chopped coarsely

4 green onions, chopped coarsely

2 cloves garlic, quartered

1 tablespoon coarsely grated lemon rind

1.5kg spinach, trimmed, chopped coarsely

3 large potatoes (900g), chopped coarsely

3 cups (750ml) vegetable stock

5 cups (1.25 litres) water

³/₄ cup (180ml) cream

150g fetta cheese, crumbled

MELT BUTTER in large frying pan; cook combined onions and garlic, stirring, until onions soften. Add rind, spinach and potato; cook, stirring, until spinach is just wilted.

STIR IN STOCK and the water. Bring to a boil; simmer, covered, about 15 minutes or until the potato softens.

BLEND OR PROCESS soup mixture, in batches, until smooth.

RETURN SOUP with cream to same cleaned pan; stir over heat until hot. Divide soup among serving bowls; top each with cheese.

Serves 6.

citrus fruit

VALENCIA ORANGES HANGING ON WITH
THE NEW SPRING BLOSSOMS

Delightful is the heavy drape of white blooms among lustrous, deep green foliage. Throughout spring that distinctive citrus perfume pervades the air and sends bees into overtime on nectar-gathering scurries. By autumn the branches arch gracefully and bow down laden with fruit.

The fruits are legendary: filled with juice and bursting with flavour. They are also decorative and long lasting, both on the tree and when chilled for storage. When not used for eating fresh or for their juice, the various fruits can be used in pickles or chutneys, salted as a condiment or sweetened for marmalades or desserts. As a bonus, they are full of vitamins.

Honestly, how have you managed without a citrus tree?

general cultivation

Citrus trees require free-draining soil. Where clay is the base layer or chief component of the soil, the water will drain away too slowly and the roots will rot. To plant a citrus tree in these soils, first apply gypsum to the surface, then follow with a mixture of sand and straw, then raise the soil 30cm (12") with a mixture of rotted manure, sand and compost. Let this rest for 2 weeks before planting.

To keep all citrus trees in top form, spread a special citrus-blend fertiliser or a combination of pelleted poultry manure and fish-food fertiliser in late winter or early spring and again in late summer. Water in well. The roots lie close to the surface, spreading out to the drip-line of each tree, so avoid disturbing the soil.

Mulch with compost or lucerne hay to retain moisture but keep it well clear of the trunk. Apply fertiliser under the drip-line and water in well. Collar rot around the base of the trunk occurs from damp foliage and the build up of too much mulch around the stem. Always keep this area clear.

Water regularly for good flower and fruit formation. Don't let the roots dry out during long, dry spells. Watering is especially important for trees in pots, and an automatic watering system is very effective.

Most purchased citrus trees are grafted onto hardy, disease-resistant rootstock. Never bury the tree as deep as the graft when planting or adding mulch. Keep a check that new stems don't shoot below the graft as this is the rootstock growing. The vigorous rootstock can rapidly overcome the grafted variety. If growing from seed, buy "certified seed" to guarantee the variety you want.

Citrus don't like frosts or exposure to cold gales, and in cold climates they are grown in conservatories. If grown in pots, they can be moved outdoors in warm weather, but in-ground specimens need wide open doorways during warm weather for air circulation and bees. Protected by a wall or within a courtyard, some citrus varieties cope with light frosts.

Citrus trees, unpruned, naturally assume a neat, compact shape. Lemon trees become open and wide-armed in full sun. Should their spread become too generous, they happily adapt to pruning back into their natural shape. Hard pruning can be used to re-invigorate an old tree. Cut back to a few short stubs of branches at the main trunk. Citrus trees can also be pruned as topiary balls at ground level or standardised on self-supporting trunks.

Remember to leave the fruit on the tree until fully ripe and ready to fall as it doesn't ripen after picking.

pests and diseases

Any discolouration or yellowing in the normally glossy evergreen foliage tells you that something in the soil is amiss, usually a lack of trace elements. The correct fertiliser regime is called for. Your nursery can diagnose the problem.

Holes bitten in the leaves are a minor problem caused by snails or caterpillars which can be removed by hand. More disfiguring are leaf miners that make tracks just below the leaf surface and pucker the entire leaf. They can be clipped off or sprayed with white oil mix in late winter and again in summer. Watch for new leaves unfurling and spray immediately.

Aphids will mass on new stems and leaves, and disfigure or kill them. Crush by hand, hose off or spray with an insecticide. See page 9 for safe spray alternatives. A black mould, sooty mould, can appear on stems and leaves from the honeydew dropped by scale and aphids. Lightly sponge off with warm, soapy water and search for and remove the honeydew producers.

Another visitor is the destructive bronze-orange bug that starts life in winter as a flat, paper-thin beetle. It grows and changes to green then orange. It is easily visible in its final black-bronze stage when it's almost 3cm (1") long and sucks from the ends of new stems. The stems wilt and the bug squirts a burning liquid with an unpleasant aroma when disturbed. Use a proprietary spray or don rubber gloves and protective glasses and catch them one by one and crush or dip into a hot water bath to destroy.

Scales, with their white, pink or brown round waxy coatings or fine desiccated coconut appearance, also mass on the stems of citrus trees. They suck out vital fluids and are very weakening. Proprietary treatments are available. Alternatively, they can be removed with gentle scrubbing with a soft brush.

Fruit fall is another common problem and is usually related to irregular watering. Another reason may be spined citrus bugs, flattened green beetles with horns on either side of their flat heads. They suck from the immature fruits. Treatment is the same as for bronze-orange bugs.

'NAGAMI' CUMQUAT

North African recipes often call for preserved lemons. Quarter lemons lengthways and place in sterilised jars (see Bottling, page 118) with salt and sugar; add flavourings such as cinnamon sticks, peppercorns, cumin seeds and bay leaves and cover the lemons with fresh lemon juice. Keep in the refrigerator for up to 6 months. To use, remove and discard the pulp. Slice the rind finely and serve over dishes. Note: the juice is not suitable to use as it's too salty.

PRESERVING THE CROP

STORING Citrus fruits should be stored in a cool, dry place for up to 3 weeks. Storing in the refrigerator will slightly lengthen their shelf life.

FREEZING Both the rind and juice freeze well. Remove the rind before freezing and store in plastic containers ready to use. Juice can be frozen in small amounts, such as ice-cube trays, then transferred to freezer bags once frozen (see Freezing, page 117). Freeze juice and rind for up to 6 months. Cumquats and lemons can be frozen whole, packed into rigid freezer containers, for up to 6 months. You will not be able to grate the rind once it has defrosted, but the lemons can still be juiced and the cumquats used as desired. Frozen lemon slices can be added to summer drinks.

PICKLING All citrus fruits make excellent jams, jellies and marmalades. Pour into hot, sterilised jars and seal while hot (see Bottling, page 118).

KAFFIR LIMES AND THEIR TWO-PART LEAVES

in the garden

oranges

Oranges crop for 3–4 months over winter and into spring. Valencia has seeds and a tough skin but is an excellent orange for juice. Navel oranges are the most popular eating orange with no pips, lots of juice and are easy to peel. They ripen in winter and their bright, vitamin-packed flesh is a real fillip. Blood oranges, with their streaky red flesh, are startling when cut, and the bitter Seville orange is excellent for marmalade and candying. Calamondin, a dwarf sweet orange, and Chinotto, a bitter one, look good in pots.

lemons

Lemon trees make ideal cook's companions as they are rarely without fruit. During winter the crop is most abundant, ready for marmalades, salting, juicing and freezing. Lemon is the tallest and most rambling member of the citrus troupe but responds happily to pruning and shaping.

'Eureka' is productive all year in mild climates. 'Meyer' is suitable for areas of light frosts and adapts well to pots. 'Lisbon' only crops once a year. A newer cultivar named the 'Lemonade Tree' has a sweeter, less acidic juice.

limes

Lime trees are more compact than lemons. Most varieties hold some fruit all year, but winter is their peak season. They are the most frost-sensitive of all citrus trees. Kaffir limes are grown for their aromatic leaves and zest. Native finger limes produce caviar-like balls of lime.

mandarins and tangerines

These crop once a year from late autumn to winter. Don't leave the fruit too long before picking as they dry out on the tree. Leave some stem attached if you plan to store them. Easy-to-peel mandarin varieties include 'Imperial'. Seedless varieties include 'Emperor'. Cross-breeds of mandarin and orange have produced the tangor, and mandarin/grapefruit crosses have produced the tangy tangelo.

grapefruit

That clean, sharp taste is a robust start to the day. Grapefruit appear once a year, in either autumn ('Wheeny') or winter ('Marsh Seedless'). In Britain, 'Golden Special' is prized, and pink and blood grapefruits are becoming a garden must. Grapefruit are prone to fruit-fly attack, so treat as advised (see page 9). Bag the fallen fruit, "cook" it in the sun and dispose of carefully.

cumquats

These ornamental trees have miniature fruit and leaves. The oval-fruited 'Nagami' has fewer seeds and sweet flesh concealed in a thin, bitter skin. 'Marumi' has round fruit and sharp-flavoured flesh. A variegated form is also available. Cumquats make distinctive marmalade as well as citrus-based liqueurs.

for the table

to prepare...

 To remove the rind and pith from thick-rind fruit: top and tail the fruit, then slit the skin from top to bottom. Gently work a spoon under the skin and around the fruit. You will end up with rind ready for making into sweet treats and rind-free fruit ready to cook with or enjoy as they are.

to serve...

 There is, of course, their juice to enjoy.

 When not eaten fresh or used for their juice, most members of the citrus family can be used in pickles or chutneys, salted as a condiment or sweetened for marmalades or desserts.

 Serve butter, grated mandarin rind and a little five-spice powder over steamed bok choy.

 Remove the white pith from the rind of your chosen citrus fruit. Make sure the rind is dried thoroughly (see Drying, page 119), then place in jars of caster sugar. Limit yourself to one flavour per jar. After a month the sugar is wonderfully scented with the fruit and ready to add to sweet batters.

 Combine avocados, grapefruit segments and butter lettuce; toss with a spicy dressing made with grapefruit juice

 To add extra zing to casseroles and slow-cooked meats, sprinkle with gremolata (a mixture of garlic, lemon rind and parsley). Excellent with veal, beef or grilled fish.

 Dust plenty of icing sugar onto a cake straight from the oven and squeeze over citrus juice: a good alternative to pouring over a sugar syrup.

never-lasting orange slices

These orange slices can be used in trifles, cake fillings, as cheesecake toppings or even squeezed into split croissants for a special breakfast. They will keep in the refrigerator for up to 6 months, if they last that long.

12 medium oranges (2.2kg)

10 cups (2.5 litres) water

8 cups (1.75kg) caster sugar

³/₄ cup (180ml) orange-flavoured liqueur

BRING A VERY LARGE PAN of salted water to the boil; add the whole oranges. Return to the boil; drain, rinse under cold water. Repeat twice more. Cut oranges into 5–7mm (¹/₄") thick slices, removing the seeds.

COMBINE WATER and sugar in a very large pan. Stir over heat until sugar is dissolved; do not boil. Add the orange slices and simmer for about 2 hours or until the orange slices are soft and very shiny. Stir in liqueur. Gently spoon slices into hot sterilised jars (see Bottling, page 118) and seal while hot.

If you have a lot of syrup leftover, you can bottle some separately to spoon over cakes or flavour creams.

winter herbs

FORMAL STANDARD BAY AMONG A RIOT OF GARDEN

PRESERVING THE CROP

STORING Store fresh herbs in damp paper towel in vegetable storage bags in the refrigerator for up to 3 days.

FREEZING Bay leaves, thyme, marjoram and sage all freeze well. Freeze in small containers for up to 6 months (see Freezing, page 117). They don't need to be chopped before freezing; freeze in a covered tray with their stems intact. Frozen, the leaves are easily removed to use.

DRYING All the winter herbs can be dried and stored in airtight containers for several months (see Drying, page 119). Hang bunches decoratively around the kitchen.

The perennial herbs available to us in the winter enjoy an uncanny sympathy with the foods we crave when the nights turn cold and dark: roasts, soups, dishes that require long cooking which draws out flavours and fills the house with rich scents and fireside warmth. Summer seems a long way off, and winter herbs capture that absent sunshine.

in the garden

bay

Bay is one of the few tree herbs. And what a tree! It's not choosy about soils or climate and it can reach 11m (35') and spread almost as wide. A bay tree is more suited to a large garden or park rather than a herb patch, but it adapts to topiary shaping and is often standardised as feature points in the centre or corners of a formal garden. Bay also grows well in a pot, and can be espaliered as a hedge, fence or border.

The leathery evergreen leaves are used to flavour casseroles, milk sauces, stock and marinades. Dry and store in an airtight container. They can be used fresh, but some people insist the flavour is stronger when dried.

Watch for brown scale on the leaves because *en masse* they can weaken a small tree. Lightly scrub them off with soapy water or use a proprietary spray.

thyme

This low-growing herb is excellent in the garden as a border, in clumps among rocks or in pots. It needs full sun and gritty, free-draining soil to thrive. It will rot in damp, shady sites. It grows to about 30cm (12") but it usually masses on itself and leans over and sets roots. Cut it back when it gets too unmanageable and use the new rooted plants as replacements every couple of years. There are many leaf forms and varieties which are used fresh and dried. Lemon thyme goes particularly well with mushrooms and veal. Add thyme at the beginning of cooking so the flavours meld. Pull off the small leaves if you don't want to serve them with their stringy stems.

marjoram

Marjoram is a relative of oregano; grows lower at about 30cm (12") and its spread is more of a mound. Their flavours are similar. Marjoram will sulk and disappear in shady spots and needs protection from cold winter winds. It is well suited to life in a pot. Prune back hard at the end of summer and collect the trimmings to dry. Marjoram teams well with tomato-based dishes and the dried stems burnt on the barbecue add a tang to food.

sage

There are handsome purple-flushed and yellow-variegated sages available as well as the usual grey. Sage grows about 30cm (12") high, doesn't grow in acidic soil and will collapse with too much rain. Add dolomite to the soil if you've had failures before, and confinement to a well-drained pot will reduce "wet feet" syndrome. Watch for caterpillars as they'll strip the leaves in no time. Its deep blue salvia flowers appear in spring, but for profuse leaves, snip off the stems as the flowers form. The flavour of sage is strong, fresh or dried, so use sparingly. The intense flavour suits strongly flavoured dishes such as pork and duck.

for the table

to serve...

⤳ BAY leaves are said to ward off weevils so scatter through your pantry. Even if this doesn't work, the leaves will add a wonderful scent to the shelves.

⤳ Cook crumbed lamb cutlets in butter and oil; remove from pan and add lemon juice, THYME and more butter. Serve the butter sauce over the lamb.

⤳ Squeeze lemon juice and sprinkle chopped fresh MARJORAM over potatoes before roasting. The smell and flavour are both delicious.

⤳ Place a SAGE leaf and a piece of mozzarella in the centre of a pork schnitzel; fold into parcels, secure with string; dust in flour and cook in butter and olive oil until golden and cooked through. Remove the string before serving.

ELEGANT GREY-LEAFED SAGE

braised pork with fresh sage

1.5kg rack of pork (6 cutlets)

90g butter

2 medium carrots (240g), thickly sliced

6 baby onions (150g), peeled

4 cloves garlic, peeled

2 bay leaves

6 sprigs fresh thyme

1¹/₃ cups (330ml) white wine

15g butter, extra

1 tablespoon plain flour

1 tablespoon sage leaves

MELT BUTTER in a large, flameproof dish. Add pork and brown all sides; remove. Add carrots, onions, garlic, bay leaves and thyme to dish. Stir over heat for 5 minutes or until beginning to brown. Return pork to dish with wine. Transfer to moderate oven for about 1¹/₄ hours or until cooked as desired. Remove pork; keep warm.

STRAIN cooking liquid, discarding vegetables. Bring liquid to boil; whisk in extra butter blended with the flour, boil until slightly thickened. Stir in sage. Serve pork with sage sauce.

Serves 6.

Ask your butcher to remove the rind and tie the pork well. Roast the salted rind on a rack in a hot oven until crisp. Serve with the pork.

saving
the season's abundance

One danger of successful gardening is sheer over-abundance. What do you do with kilos of zucchinis? Mint gone mad? Too many beans?

One of the delights of too-successful gardening is preserving the crop, giving away what you don't need, storing for winter, making gifts, and enjoying last year's apricots, oranges and tomatoes as this year's jams, marmalades and preserves.

Here we provide you with general guidelines on simple home preservation techniques. Always choose the best, the ripest and the least blemished of your fruit and vegetables. And don't leave preserving until the season's end or you will miss the best of your crop.

freezing

Containers must be airtight. Shallow dishes allow food to freeze and thaw more quickly. Containers must be microwave-safe if you plan to microwave from the freezer. Always allow cooked food to cool completely before freezing. Food expands as it freezes so allow 2–5cm (1–2") extra space in containers.

Use labels to record the contents, freezing date and quantity. Remember to use a waterproof pen.

Ice-cube trays are perfect containers for freezing small quantities – chopped herbs, citrus rind, juice, chopped chillies, chopped lemon grass, grated ginger and passionfruit pulp. Each compartment holds about 1 tablespoon. Some herbs may need a little water to cling together. Once frozen, transfer the cubes to a container or bag. Each time you need the flavouring, add a cube!

Sprigs of herbs can be crumbled while still frozen. Basil, mint, oregano and coriander freeze well. Once frozen, herbs are only useful in cooked dishes or salad dressings, not as salad ingredients.

To blanch vegetables before freezing, drop them into a large pan of boiling water and allow the water to return to the boil. Drain immediately and plunge into a large bowl (or sink) of iced water until cold. Drain well before packing into freezer containers. If blanching large quantities, check the temperature of the iced water as it does warm up. Add more iced water, if necessary.

Frozen stone fruit, apples, pears and oranges make quick desserts. Poach in a light sugar syrup with spices and freeze in rigid containers to keep their shape. To serve, thaw and spoon over ice-cream or freshly baked plain cakes.

PHOTO: SCOTT CAMERON

FOOD	FREEZER LIFE (months at -18°C)
Berries, raw	24
Stone fruit, raw	18
Asparagus, blanched	12
Green beans, blanched	15
Brussels sprouts, blanched	15
Carrots, blanched	18
Corn cobs	10
Herbs, fresh	6

STERILISING JARS

There are three main methods of home sterilisation. Once sterilised, remove each jar carefully and turn upside-down onto a clean tea-towel on a wooden board. Turn upright only when ready to use.

METHOD 1 This is by far the easiest method. Put the jars and lids in the dishwasher on the hottest rinse cycle available. Don't use detergent.

METHOD 2 Lay the jars and lids in a large pan, cover completely with cold water and bring gradually to boil. Boil for 20 minutes.

METHOD 3 Place the jars and lids, upright, but not touching on a clean wooden board. Place the board in a cold oven and turn the temperature to very low for 30 minutes.

PHOTOS: AWW HOME LIBRARY

bottling

Old-fashioned bottling requires a bottling kit, a set of instructions and years of experience. Some practitioners have turned bottling into an art (visit any country show), but the technique is complex and not for the beginner or those rushed for time. If you want to try bottling, seek the help of a friend or relative with experience in this method of preservation.

Making preserves (jam, pickles, chutneys, relishes) is a much simpler alternative to bottling. The added sugar and vinegar act as preservation agents, lessening the need for precise temperatures and heating times. Follow our instructions for sterilising and sealing bottles and preserving will be easy.

Successful preservation requires still-warm, sterilised bottles, warm preserves and rapid sealing.

You'll need plenty of glass jars or bottles. They must have no chips or cracks and should be thoroughly scrubbed clean. Choose bottles with airtight, coated metal lids. Uncoated lids will corrode. Snap-on and screwtop plastic lids do not seal tightly enough.

Remember that lids need to be sterilised along with the bottles before use.

sealing jars

Sealing the jars is as important as sterilising them. Once you've filled the jars, seal them immediately. The sooner jars are sealed, the less likely are their contents to spoil.

Paper, cellophane and foil are not suitable sealants. Paper and cellophane are not airtight and foil corrodes with any acids in the preserves. Brown paper can be used as an extra sealant. When you have placed the lids on the jars, cut out a large circle of brown paper, coat with glue and place over the lids and wrap down the sides of the jar to form a tight seal.

If you don't have enough lids, use paraffin wax. It is readily available from chemists and creates an excellent seal. Melt the wax over very low heat. Pour a thin layer over the preserves and allow to set. Next, pour over another layer of wax, this time including a piece of string to help you pull out the wax to open. Don't overheat the wax or it will shrink when it sets and not form a complete seal.

labelling jars

Next step: label! Don't kid yourself you'll remember that the date and apple chutney has the green lid and the tomato cumin relish is in the tall thin bottle. Label with contents and preserving date.

Store your preserves in a cool, dark place and leave for a week or so before opening. All preserves taste better when left to rest. In hot, humid climates, the best place to store them is the refrigerator. Once opened, all preserves must be stored, covered, in the refrigerator.

drying

sun-drying

Tomatoes, apples, pears, apricots, peaches and chillies are all good to dry. You need 4–5 days of constant sun with little or no humidity. Beware: in humid conditions a mould develops very quickly. Don't be disappointed if the fruit changes colour as it dries; its taste is not affected. Commercially dried fruits have sulphur and ascorbic acid added to retain their colour. It's not necessary to peel fruit before drying, but as drying can make the skin leathery (apples and apricots in particular), you may wish to peel some fruits.

You will need wooden or non-corrosive racks with rungs close enough together to stop the food falling through (as it shrinks greatly), but not too close to disrupt airflow.

Thicker fruit, such as apples and pears, needs to be sliced; most other fruits just need halving. Place the fruit, cut-side up, on the racks, place the racks over a tray and cover with fine wire mesh (not touching the fruit). Clean fly-screens are ideal. Position in the hottest, sunniest place you can find.

It's a good idea to bring the trays inside or into an airy shed at night so they're not disturbed by animals and dew won't rehydrate the fruit and make it go mouldy. The fruit is dry when no moisture oozes when cut. Store in airtight containers in a cool place for 6 months. Of course, label as you go.

air-drying

Fresh herbs and chillies can be air-dried. Hang bunches in an airy place or on racks covered with absorbent paper, away from direct sunlight to retain as much flavour as possible.

microwave-drying

You can also dry herbs in the microwave between several sheets of absorbent paper on HIGH (100%) for about 1 minute. If not dry, repeat, checking every 30 seconds (sometimes the paper will need to be changed). Label and store in airtight containers.

oven-drying

All fruits that can be sun-dried can also be oven-dried – especially tomatoes. Prepare the fruit on racks as for sun-drying (without the fly-screen)!

A good slow drying oven temperature is about 50°C (120°F). Tomatoes need a higher temperature to dry out their extra juice. Don't hurry the process or you will spoil the fruit. You may need more than a day, so place as much fruit in the oven as you can. You can dry different fruits together. Once the fruit is dried, let it cool before storing in airtight containers.

Herbs dry very well in the oven and take little space and time (about 20 minutes), so are ideal to do in batches along with other fruit. That excess of chillies can be oven-dried as well.

PHOTO: SCOTT CAMERON

SUN-DRIED PEAR SLICES

PHOTO: ALAN BENSON

BUNCHES OF AIR-DRIED HERBS

index

oven temperatures

These oven temperatures are a guide only.

	°C (Celsius)	°F (Fahrenheit)	gas mark
very slow	120	250	1
slow	150	300	2
moderately slow	160	325	3
moderate	180-190	350-375	4
moderately hot	200-210	400-425	5
hot	220-230	450-475	6
very hot	240-250	500-525	7

Note: One Australian metric tablespoon holds 20ml. North America, NZ and the UK use 15ml tablespoons. All cup and spoon measurements are level.